RABBIT

GW01417560

By

H. D. H. Dowle.

First published privately by the Author
in 1959 at Adisham, Canterbury, Kent.

2nd Edition revised by
J.C.Sandford & Joyce Potter

1992

Copyright 1992 by
The Coney Press
10, Hengist Way,
Bromley,
Kent. BR2 0NS

First published 1957
Revised edition 1992

ISBN 1 8980 1501 5

Printed and bound in Great Britain
by Printing for Pleasure Ltd.
Chattisham, Ipswich,
Suffolk. IP8 3QE

Preface.

The first edition of Rabbit Judgeship was written by Harold Dowle over more than five years commencing in 1953. It was intended as one of a series to be published on all aspects of the Rabbit Fancy and Rabbit Keeping. Unfortunately the series was not continued and Harold [with one of the editors] took the decision to print and publish it privately.

The book met with considerable success, and the 600 then printed were soon out of print. Plans to reprint a revised and enlarged edition were interrupted by his tragic death in 1962.

To both editors, Harold was a dear friend, and over a period of 21 years in one case and 13 in the other, discussed the philosophies and practices of judging on innumerable occasions.

The least possible changes have been made in the original wording of the author and then only when additional clarity is essential. A Memoir has been added, together with a short appendix in which comments are made on some present days practices which regrettably occasionally occur. All the points mentioned are those on which the opinion of Harold Dowle is known. Even if he had not expressed them in quite the same way, he would most certainly have approved of the sentiments.

Times have changed. In the 1940's, 50's, and 60's, when Harold had become certainly one of the leading and outstanding judges, many shows were larger than they are today and of course there were many box and table shows. There were often several judges of each section in a show, who, because of the demand for judges and the larger classes, became more quickly experienced. Travel was cheaper and novice judges found much employment in the smaller shows. But no matter what changes have occurred, the principles laid down by Harold Dowle have not changed and will continue as long as good rabbit judging continues.

Harold Dowle was a strong believer in the training at least, and preferably also, the examination of judges. His suggestions made frequently in person and again in this book have not even now been taken up as to the training. Perhaps one may hope that they will in future ?

J. C. Sandford
Joyce Potter

Memoir: Harold Dudley Halmer Dowle,   1898 - 1962

Harold Dowle was a man totally devoted to the Rabbit Fancy and was, for the whole of his life, a quite outstanding example of the true Fancier and Rabbit Judge.

Born on 27th March, 1898 in Canterbury [at the Millers Arms, which may have accounted for his life long abstinence from alcohol!] his parents after living for a short period at Dymchurch, moved in 1904 to Adisham, some 6 miles from Canterbury in Kent, where he lived for the rest of his life and there gained local fame as both a cricketer and footballer..

After the 1914-18 war in which he served first with the Royal Naval Air Service and then with the Royal Flying Corps, he married Ellen Kate Best [known all her life as Nellie], on 22nd November 1922.

His interests in football and cricket continued after his marriage and he achieved success by playing for Adisham until the 1940's when he stopped playing cricket;   football he had stopped a few years earlier. He then played a little tennis and was also very good at table tennis.

He loved, in his own words, "sloppy love stories" and was a particular fan of Netta Muskett an author of that period who wrote particularly remarkable examples of those stories.

Harold was a religious man and not only attended Baptists Chapel every Sunday but lived his life on the fullest of Christian principles.

In his professional life [and one must confess that that was when he could spare the time from rabbits and the Fancy !] he was a motor engineer and driving Instructor. He was a wonderful teacher and taught almost the entire population of Adisham to drive. He owned a small garage but it was never completely successful. For much of the time his major work was the charging of batteries, but he also collected chassis from Birmingham for coach building by Barratts of Canterbury. After the war the repair of farm machinery became a substantial part of the work.

It was, however, to rabbits that Harold was devoted. The love affair with them began after the first war when he first had Chinchillas and then Sables. It was however with Argentes that he really made his name as a successful breeder and indeed created and established the Argente Brun.

Harold was in many ways lucky to live close to that great Fancier Thomas Leaver who spent his life in Herne Bay, a matter of but 15 miles or so from Adisham. It was Thomas Leaver who encouraged him to Judge and it was he who taught him in the beginning.

Harold Dowle was a man of the deepest integrity and kindness. These attributes,coupled with his profound knowledge, particularly of Fur Rabbits, made him certainly one of the leading judges of his period. Into his book he put everything he knew during his more than 30 years of judging. He wanted others to learn and this was very typical of him. He gave freely of his time and expertise and was always ready to help others. Although tolerant of opposing views and always ready to listen to them, he was also a determined man and an excellent Committee member.

A member of the British Rabbit Council from its foundation in 1934 [and of the British Fur Rabbit Society before that] he first became, and remained as, a member of the Central Council, as representative for the Sable Club, in 1936 until his first election to the Executive Committee of the B.R.C. in 1946. He remained a member of the Executive Committee until his Death, but also served as Vice President in 1955, Chairman of the Council in 1962 and President in 1956 and 1957

His book, Rabbit Judgeship, is the only book in English devoted tothis subject. If for nothing else, and there is much, this at least will keep his memory ever fresh.

J. C. Sandford

THE OPEN DOOR WITH RESERVATIONS

To be a judge of rabbits in this country may not be a great achievement as far as the public is concerned. There is no set qualification to pass, no body to say 'Thou shalt not judge' if the occasion to judge presents itself to any person willing to undertake the task. But it is a great achievement to be recognised by the Fancy as a first class Rabbit Judge.

We are agreed that anyone with ambition and seeming ability for this very exacting kind of work must start somewhere, at some time, on the road to recognition as a competent and suitable individual to act in this capacity.

It is also generally agreed that before anybody accepts the responsibility of making the awards in a class of competitive rabbits, (where the decisions arrived at and the awards given are of importance to both exhibit and exhibitor), he or she should have satisfied themselves beforehand as to their capability to do sound justice to all concerned. To make an immature entry into the judging arena on personal assumptions alone, with little background, knowledge or experience of the complications involved, is to court disaster. It can bring mutual disappointment and harsh and severe comment from the offended, in sufficient force to squash even the desire to become a judge of repute.

In the past prospective judges have been left to make their own way in the struggle for recognition as best they can, with almost no help or encouragement or guidance to facilitate the effort, from official circles. Whatever the future may offer in this direction, by way of preliminary early training, it will still be up to the aspirant to take the initial step towards the objective.

SELF PREPARATION

Much can be accomplished by study alone. Study will aid proficiency in many things relating to judging before active work is taken up in earnest. Some things may only be acquired after lengthy experience in actual adjudication and do not concern us here. It is essential for the person contemplating a judge's career to gain sound knowledge of all breed standards. These standards have been drawn up, by responsible persons, with intense care and consideration to describe the ideal specimen of each particular breed, indicating the proportionate values to be placed on each of them.

The standards have been drawn up with the express purpose of guiding breeders and judges in the essential qualities required in each particular breed.

Pay particular attention to the directions in all standards regarding faults and disqualifications. Be quite clear in your mind on these points for both carry penalties for the judge to impose.

It is not necessary to memorise each and every standard in its entirety. Study every one frequently to keep the main points fresh in your mind. It will be surprising how vividly they flash to memory when needed if sufficient attention has been given in this direction.

It is not always possible to determine the correct impression intended by simply reading the description of a breed. In fact the word picture of any rabbit is usually something of a mystery to anyone who is not familiar with a living specimen. To gain the right conception, make a comparison between the written ideal and the live rabbit with someone having practical knowledge of the breed concerned. The specialist breeder is fully alive to the meaning of the words used in the description of his breed and will be of great help in clearing preconceived ideas from your mind should they be incorrect. Do not be content with a single opinion on a breed standard; seek as many as you can. You will find slight variations between breeders on some points, but these differences will be invaluable in the formation of a balanced outlook.

Carry this kind of self education to as many of the breeds as is possible. You should cover the entire range. Go out of your way to make contacts and visit the rabbitries where quality stock is bred. You can never learn too much of rabbit characteristics from the judging angle.

In adopting this procedure you will have time to be thorough in your comparison of stock with its standard of excellence, and it will give you a better chance to get the undivided attention of the breeder than you would get at any show where time is always at a premium. Serious conversation is subject to all sorts of interruption during show time, often just at the crucial moment when it could have been a good fact finding opportunity.

You may have no intention of becoming an all round judge, and might think the suggestion of covering all standards in preliminary preparation too comprehensive an undertaking to bother with. However, no matter in which of the sections, Fancy, Normal Fur, or Rex, you wish to make a career, when you do eventually commence judging, before you get far on the road the Any Variety class in one form or another will come your way. Any variety classes are some of the most difficult in which to dispense justice and even more importantly you will be required to co-judge the Breeders and Challenge Classes. The other section judge will most likely be more knowledgeable on the finer points of the standards of those breeds. If you have neglected to study the standard of one of the breeds therein you cannot give it proper consideration in making the awards.

The importance of full knowledge of the standards and their relationship to the breeds cannot be over emphasised. Unless there is a good measure of uniformity of ideas and the interpretation of standards between the breeder and the judge, the issue will not be congenial to either.

SHOW RULES

Show rules should be an early focal point for consideration as all worth-while Shows are held under the Rules of the British Rabbit Council. The Show Rules section is extensive and definite in object and design. It covers almost every phase of exhibiting; the rabbit, the exhibitor, the steward, and the judge.

The judge is the person in charge of the proceedings, and it is his responsibility to see that there is no infringement of rules by animal or person. All judges must read, mark and learn these rules to the best of their understanding. To be well versed in this section adds greatly to efficiency in judging. To be expert in breed lore, capable in making awards acceptable to the majority interested in them, but with uncertainty in show rules and regulations, is to miss the full acquirement expected of you.

Show rules, in the main, are suggestions from the exhibiting public, based on actual happenings at shows. They are considered by the Annual General Meeting of the British Rabbit Council and finally ratified by the members in the ballot, before being put into operation. Therefore they are liable to alteration, modification and change from time to time in order to improve competitive conditions.

If a judge is not up-to-date in this field he, or she, may

unwittingly be guilty of error, thereby inflicting hardship on one exhibitor and misleading another. This may cause complications difficult to overcome.

Particular attention should be given to the conditions governing the award of Challenge Certificates and Diplomas offered by the B.R.C.. These valuable specials are eagerly sought after by the Association's members. If one is wrongly given to an exhibit endless trouble is caused to everybody concerned. The breed or the variety of breed entitled to compete for specific C.C.'s can be quite complicated. The general principles covering the award of C.C.'s is now fairly straight forward, when a full range is available. Restricted classification cuts down the number of C.C.'s in many cases, bringing a group of rabbits within the scope of one. Correct grouping may need more than a casual reference to avoid a mistake when allocation takes place.

Under the Show Rule heading there are several class definitions worthy of special consideration. They relate to classes restricted to certain exhibits, either by ownership, show record, or requiring balanced qualities to form a class unit. To quote, for example, 'Pairs and Teams' - a pair must consist of two rabbits, and a team of three rabbits, of the same variety, matched as closely as possible in size, colour, etc. The sex, unless specially stated in the schedule, is optional.

It is surprising how often ineligible exhibits are allowed to pass through a class without penalty, in some cases even to figure in the awards. This sort of thing does not happen through sheer ignorance. It is due to carelessness and lack of insight to responsibility.

Show Rules are therefore instructive to the judge in what must, what can and what cannot be done, whilst acting in an official capacity. The candidate judge must familiarise himself with the clear guidance given therein before attempting practical work.

Study must continue within the breeds so that you can define each one to its correct section, ie. Fancy, Normal Fur, or Rex. The more popular Fancy and Normal Fur breeds may not present difficulty. It is the rarer breeds of the two sections that can be misplaced. The Rexes identify themselves without much trouble, though the rough coated varieties have a stipulation attached which restricts their activity in general competition with the standard or smooth coated Rex. The appendix at the end of their standards in the B.R.C. standards book explains how they are to be treated. The true Satin, normal or rex, is distinct in coat finish and should not baffle the observant as to its identity.

All rabbits exhibited at Shows held under B.R.C. rules must be ringed with the appropriate sized rings, although there are a few exceptions to this general rule. The exceptions and the breed sizes should be a major concern for mind retention.

Queries arise quite frequently in these matters during judging and can be dealt with firmly without argument, if you can adopt a positive attitude, free from hesitation.

The several pointers indicated have the intention of drawing attention to the many factors prevalent in show life which affect judges actions and which can be learnt at the beginning by study alone with no need for, perhaps costly, experience. Take advantage of this asset, it is well worth the effort.

GLEANINGS FROM THE SHOWS

The practical side of judging can only be seen to profit at shows where a full selection of the breeds is catered for, and the conditions ideal for observation.

The small Table Show [although at the present time, 1992, there are very few] had a value in bringing on the possible judge, but to the early beginner it sometimes created wrong impressions, owing to its limitations in time, number of exhibits of the same kind in competition, and the short time any rabbit was on view. All things were minimised at these events. The animals were tabled, judged and boxed. Interest in the majority finished with one brief operation.

At the open Pen Show all exhibits can be seen and examined visually during the show. This enables the order of awards to be followed as the officiating judge has placed them. They may not be in accord with the onlookers ideas, as viewing alone cannot produce a conclusive estimate of merit, but it gives food for thought as to why one exhibit is placed in front of the other, and is conducive to self-reasoning.

To get the most helpful insight as to what is taking place, a hand should be given with the stewarding. Act as a steward on every conceivable occasion. This brings more direct contact with the judge and the methods employed in dealing with a class of rabbits. When giving assistance at the judging table the steward will get a close up sight, under actual conditions prevailing at the time of assessment. This has a definite advantage over pen side noting. The exhibits are bound to change position several times during the judge's examination, especially if the class is fairly level in quality.

Try reasoning in your own mind, with the reasoning of the judge. You may be quite a bit out in predicting the final placings, but it is good educational eye training to quickly spot the most probables.

After a period of general stewarding duties it will be comparatively easy to move a step nearer to the scene of your intention by doing service as the Judges book steward.

The book steward and his work are not defined by B.R.C. rules, but no judge dispenses with this helpful assistant unless forced to do so by reason of a steward shortage. A competent person in this capacity can save the judge much of the routine detail work connected with the judging book. Checking exhibits on and off the table, dealing with the ear-label bug-bear, recording the ring number of the winner as read out by the Judge, and so on. This service rendered faithfully, allows the judge some slight relaxation between classes, and is gratefully appreciated.

As a book steward, you are what is termed by exhibitors 'on the other side of the table', and that much nearer to the judging. Here, all things seen from the opposite side can still be seen, but with keeness on your part, the finer points in regard to requirements in a particular breed, or otherwise, as uncovered by the judge in minute searching, may be perceived. Make mental notes on presumed judgement of slight failings or glaring faults and the good points. This will enable you to check your own anticipation and any failing in it, against the expert. The position the rabbit occupies in the class when judging is over is officially correct.

Carry on in this way when and where you can. Select different judges to work under. Change the sections from Fancy to Fur to Rex. It will add to your experience and instruction. Use discretion in the work, but do not be afraid to ask questions of the judge you assist as to why this or that was done, or what points separated two very close rivals. Most judges will give a satisfactory answer, with clear explanation, to the genuine enquiry. This type of stewarding is one of the best object lessons open to the student judge, when the judge is in the top rank category.

DISCRETION IN OBSERVATION

No judge, however popular, is one hundred per cent perfect in judging technique, especially when carrying out the work in the average general way, which, more often that not, is being done within a time limit. This should be kept in mind when seeking the best things from someone's actions, to aid your efficiency for the future. Remember also that the adjudicator is unconscious of your interest in every move as an example.   To do something expeditiously and to do the same thing as a demonstration would produce a quite different effect.

Craftsmanship is subject to definite correctness in its application. The craftsman, in the light of full experience, may and very often will, deviate from the set rules in applying practical skill, with no detriment to prestige or the final result.   The apprentice to a craft must adhere to the fundamentals of it, if he or she is to become master of the work, until such time as proficiency will permit a short cut which can be taken in some direction without adverse consequences.

In watching the various etiquettes in judging closely, you will be able to detect the good from the bad practices without difficulty. Retain only first class actions which appeal to your sense as highly commendable. Reject all others as unworthy of the slightest consideration. In this way you will build your future judging conduct on the good points displayed by many persons in the profession.

The rising rabbit judge should strive to surpass present day judges in the exemplary discharge of all actions subsidiary to actual decisions. Make this your aim and you will at least maintain present standards. To know the rudiments of good judging is a sound foundation and most valuable to advancement, but there are other qualifications needed if you are to succeed conclusively as a leading personage in the pursuit. Many of these points will be made clear to the reader as other aspects of judging are dealt with.

It will not be out of place here, however, to make brief reference to proposals put forward from several sides of the fancy which are interested in judges and judging evolution. The main suggestion is that the leading Judges today, who are almost continually active, should coach some of the younger persons who have a seeming flair for judging. In short the judges should act as tutor to a pupil when going about their business from show to show.

This principle may sound ideal, but it is quite impracticable. When serious consideration is given to all that the judge has to contend with in carrying through an engagement, it will be seen that there is no room for distraction, other than the unavoidable ones. Something might, and indeed ought to be done to assist entry into the judging circle when the merit of the recruit is evident. The inauguration of a scheme for practical instruction in judging should not be too great an enterprise for the 'Main Body in Rabbit Control' to arrange and support.

The need for some kind of order in preliminary training is more pressing now than ever before. With the increase in the number of breeds, varieties and show rules and regulations, it must be bewildering for the novice judge at the start.

How much responsibility lays with the judge of high standing in the furtherance of a possible judging successor's schooling is a matter of conjecture. Whatever the feeling in this matter there is no doubt that a little help is worth more than anything else to the one struggling along on lonesome initiative. Generous support by the elite to the prospective follower would, in the long run, level up judging standards all round. If a more or less fixed course were set in judging ethics, taking the broad view, the result could only benefit the judge to be, and a basic background would be prepared for future progress. Its controlled direction would obviate misguided entry into the realms of judging and ensure some uniformity in ideas for those with prospects.

In every other kind of specialisation, Professional, Sporting or Commercial, a curriculum is in being to assist preparation to ultimate graduation. All who make the grade together, in any sphere, have the same grounding and training, but apply their expertness with a difference, thus retaining individualism.

The old cry - peculiar to the Rabbit Fancy - opposing suggestions of this nature (such as 'who judges the judges') would be heard. The answer to these 'diehard critics' is that the EXPERIENCED take their lead in all things appertaining to their calling designed to higher its prestige.

THINGS OF IMPORTANCE IN THE PERSON

TEMPERAMENT

This is a quality all judges - competent or potential - must cultivate and control in the highest degree. An equable temperament is a self disciplinary act in which instruction from one individual to another can play no great part towards its development. An equable temperament is necessary to exercise restraint in word or deed, to uphold dignity, when need arises. To be cool, calm and collected in uncongenial surroundings is one great asset of immense value to a judge. No two persons are quite the same temperamentally, but some judges set a very high standard in this virtue. Their example is worth the effort to emulate in preliminary self training.

Accepting a good temperament as a virtue, it is a possession all have in a limited measure. If too limited it is liable to prove a serious drawback in judging. To have all other attributes to judge but not the disposition to apply these serenely under adverse or trying conditions is partial failure to fulfil the expectation that the people you intend to serve look for in a judge.

Nothing distracts from sound judgement so much as annoyance at a remark or act made while judging is in progress. Unfavourable reaction may divert concentration and awards from the original intention.

To be forewarned in some of the things that can upset ones equanimity is to be forearmed. Thus the obstacles marring the passage to orderly progress in judging may be avoided in so far as personal control can go. You will be the exception if, at the beginning of your active participation in serious judging, some audible remarks concerning the methods you are employing are not made. It may be in jest or for a specific purpose. Whatever the intention, do your level best to ignore the matter. Deeds may be done by someone near at hand to indicate what they would do in your position. Treat these with utter contempt.

A period of testing as to your susceptibility to distraction is inevitable early on. It is a phase in judging experience few have escaped. The reaction to it is recorded by those present and becomes part of your reputation for good or ill as long as you're remembered in the Fancy, whatever your ultimate conduct may be.

It is not always a person who disturbs the judges tranquillity. Exhibits can be most contrary on occasions, in various ways. One rabbit frisking about all over the table, creating a mild stampede is not a rarity. When this happens, endeavour to restore order without showing exasperation. Some of your stewards may be new to the job and need a little guidance from you as to how to hold and control restive stock. You should be able to do this with quiet efficiency thus giving the timid person some confidence to help hide his shortcomings.

All Stewards are only human and most do a good turn at the judging table. A lapse of attention to the work on hand, by friendly conversation one to another, will sometimes allow the already positioned placing of the class to become disarranged, making it necessary for you to repeat something you thought finished. Take it as all in the days work and refrain from harsh comment or signs of impatience. The steward's effort is voluntary, with no obligation to continue helping you under discourteous treatment. The judge cannot afford to lose valuable co-operation from helpers for that retards progress to completion of the contract.

The brief outline set out above will indicate the nature of things which can happen to fray the temper and against which you must guard. Test and examine yourself in the matter of irritability and its companions.

The right answer to these things is the assurance you must have to go forward in the project. The fiery temperament has wrecked more than one otherwise promising judging career, to my personal knowledge.

CHARACTER

The need for a judge to have an exemplary character in the light of judging responsibilities cannot be overstressed. Without it, the chance to succeed is somewhat remote. All things leading to a good reputation depend upon the full confidence of all engaged in exhibiting or show management. This confidence is especially vital in the absent exhibitor who does not accompany his stock to witness its chance for honours in the competition. These sporting supporters of the shows rely on the appointed judge to apply just dues to all exhibits, irrespective of the presence of absence or the owners.

Unless this confidence exists, free of all doubt, people with stock ready for exhibition, will not risk their time, trouble and expense entering under you. Nothing less than the even chance to win, based on quality versus quality, is acceptable.

If the slightest suspicion gets around that doubtful decisions and awards are being made by a judge, it is invariably the beginning of the end of a judging venture. The 'Bush Telegraph System' appears to be highly efficient throughout the entire rabbit Fancy. It rapidly signals doubtful doings to all parts of the British Isles, with delinquent judges well to the fore in news headlines. Something in the nature of irregularity happening in the north on one day is common gossip in the south, east and west within the week.

Fortunately, many of the penside stories touching on judges seeming misdemeanours, have little or no substance to them. Fictional exaggeration is by no means excluded from show life. The action of judges in carrying out their duties is always open to misconstruction by interested parties viewing the process.

The judge is often made a target owing to the need for an excuse by the exhibitor for missing some premier award. This particularly occurs when the exhibitor has enhanced ideas of his exhibit's merit, which may have had a series of easy wins.

The eager type of fancier, in anticipating the result, forgets that stars rise and fall with almost unfailing regularity in all branches of sporting, commercial and competitive sphere. The exhibitor, excited and expectant, often fails to recognise the opposing entrants chances in the challenge. It is generally disappointment in defeat which causes the judge to be slated, with no genuine aspersion against his character.

The judge is the only person with the right to determine positions in any class of rabbits. The advantages of minute examination before reaching decisions are obvious. The onlooker can no more than surmise values. Provided that all awards are given in strict rotation, with no partiality to man or beast, in accordance with honest conviction and dispensed in near accuracy to breed standard requirements, your character will suffer no harm from remarks made in a moment of frustration. As a judge, at classic or the smallest of shows, make this principle your firm resolve from the onset and stick to it at all costs. It would be most unwise to even contemplate deviation from the straight and narrow path of true justice as you see it. No attempt to please or favour anyone striving to gain a concession must enter your mind. Grind the axe of show records for no one, for it leads to untold complications and inglorious results for the grinder.

No judge, however experienced, thorough or popular, can entirely escape from the forces of circumstances in which the opinion given is open to dissension through petty rivalry. It must be accepted as part of the position you hold. Its offset is to be upright, straightforward, honest and unbiased in every single decision made. This is the sure way to win respect, support and tolerance from the Fancy you serve.

CONFIDENCE

Confidence is one virtue every judge must have. It goes with, and is part of, the make up of efficiency. Self confidence is necessary to carry out your task to your personal satisfaction, at the same time as imparting reasonable gratification to the others concerned with the many exacting things covering the work. To be lacking in sureness between mind and action is too great an obstacle to surmount. The handicap it places on the venture cancels out the majority of other acquisitions one may possess. So much so, in fact, as to make it well nigh futile for a start to be made in judging at the lowest scale, let alone to reach any great heights in the assembly.

There are many breeders who, although they produce the finest stock for exhibition that one could wish to see or handle, have insufficient self-confidence to judge at a show. They have no trouble in picking from their own stud the right rabbit to do full justice to their reputation as knowledgeable persons in the breed or breeds. First prize cards gained by them are sure proof of this assumption.

With this creditable skill one would think they had sufficient qualification to lead to judging excellence, at least as judges of the breeds in which they are successfully active. Yet when approached with the suggestion of judging, they frankly shrink from the very thought of it. They will admit that it is no great trouble to sort stock correctly to its approximate order of merit when they are in the quietness of their rabbitry and free from interruption and distraction and have plenty of time in which to make a decision. But to go through a class of rabbits as the official judge, in the full light of conditions prevailing at the shows, with no inkling as to the stocks good, bad or indifferent points, would simply bewilder them. The conditions appear to make it impossible for them to clarify slender separating properties in exhibits. To decide such issues under pressure would be utter confusion for them, resulting in chaotic awards.

With this class of person it is a minus in confidence which

holds back their chance to shine as a judge. The direct opposite to this short-coming is over confidence. This is dangerous and equally detrimental to sound judgement, for it can only end in blunders, grave inaccuracy and final embarrassment to the judge.

Guard against presumptuousness; it is no substitute for genuine capability. Resist the impulse to premature public display and be sure you can walk the path with rational dignity. You cannot hope to rush it. It is the quiet, calm confidence, based on the sound fundamentals within the calling, that counts. It gives assurance to all who stand or fall by the findings of the judge.

PERSONALITY

This is something peculiar to the one individual. No two judges are alike. In taking stock of it in relationship to the judges of today, we find every conceivable contrast in the personalities displayed. They are as varied as the numerous breeds and qualities in the breeds handled by them.

We cannot entirely ignore the question of personality for the rabbit community at large forever discuss the mannerisms of the judge and pass opinions on them. It is however, debatable whether it has much effect or plays any great part as an essential in the role of judge, for we find the widest variation in personalities being engaged here there and everywhere, with direct opposites working side by side at the same show.

It would appear that some fanciers have a preference for the judge who carries on quietly, without fuss or flourish. Others may favour plenty of banter and side issues tending to 'Gallery Play'. In either case, whether serious or humorous, so long as the final issue is not impaired, each one is acceptable at face value.

Be natural and courteous in all proceedings, especially to enquirers before - if its not sub vene - and after you have finished your specified duties. The exhibitors interest in a Show day and the things leading up to it are your definite concern. Treat them all with respect and personality will look after itself. Most of those with whom you come in contact with the scene of action, can appreciate that even a judge cannot altogether help, nor greatly alter, what nature has decreed in his make up.

ALACRITY

The tempo in small live stock judging, in particular with rabbits, is fast. In the main there are additional classes scheduled than were included at pre-war shows, due partly to the increase in breeds and varieties, and partly to duplicate classes. Judging was then more leisurely, but those days have gone for ever. The younger section of reigning judges adapted themselves to the increase in speed to meet the demand. The replacement judges as they fill the gaps, which will regularly appear, will have to cope likewise. There is no working to rule in this enterprise.

The average Show employing two judges means the sharing of anything from five to nine hundred entries in a comparatively short period of time, usually not exceeding six hours with a break for lunch intervening. If the ratio of three entries per exhibit is taken as a basis, it means that there are two to three hundred rabbits to be handled and overhauled thoroughly in the straight classes. Taking the lowest number of two hundred exhibits, if each judge has one half to deal with, the average time allowable for each animal is less than three minutes. This does not allow any time for the complexity of duplicate judging of one winner against another and so on, nor the time involved in the change from one class to the next.

This brief example is not far off the mark and is given to show how the need for quick action is one of the further difficulties to contend with if headway is to be gained.

The mind, hand and eye are obliged to work in unison. What the eyes see and the hands feel the mind must register automatically, otherwise a time lag ensues, which is due to the necessary consideration to balance the reactions. This would be fatal to expedient progress in the long run. The power to adjust thought, sight and touch into a single unit to accelerate judging may be partly instinctive or may be acquired through experience. Nevertheless the development of these three senses to work together, cannot be left to chance. Practice this co-ordination as a preparatory measure. To be adept in it from the start will ease the strain of anxiousness when faced with the early engagements procured. Quick and accurate is the key note in todays judging. Slowness creates irritability all round.

ENVIRONMENT

Before making the final bid for a Judge's mode of life, careful consideration should be given to the everyday affairs controlling your livelihood. The majority of Judges, past and present, have failed to grasp the exacting nature and the unseen demands involved, at the onset of the undertaking.

All the disadvantages, discomforts and inconveniences unfold their ugly heads just as soon as one begins to move out and about in fulfilment of engagements. These can upset the most careful plans laid to complete a commitment. The missing of a train on the return journey home may mean considerable delays. Inclement weather, fog or snow, can delay one for hours. If you are not more or less master of your own destiny, the risk you take in following a judging career can easily prejudice other means of security on which you depend as a mainstay of life. In some cases a superior may be willing to sanction unlimited leave of absence if he is sympathetic to the cause. If so, then you are fortunate.

The point to remember here, is that unless you are in a favourable position to have the free time in which to undertake all judging invitations that may be offered (subject to being not similarly engaged) you are at a distinct disadvantage in reaching the topmost grade.

You cannot be renowned if you are confined to a certain area by reason of circumstances, however much your ability is appreciated locally. Freedom of availability as a means to the end cannot be over emphasised. Without it, the temptation to take 'french leave' may jeopardise real substance in reaching for the precarious.

The time is not yet when the rabbit Judge can depend on the amount received in fees from engagements to provide his daily bread, no matter how great the demand for his services may be. The incentive to judge is something greater than financial reward. If finance were the only inducement to judging, then replacement judges would be one of the Fancy's biggest headaches. It is not the intention to deter anyone from a judging objective by the immediate foregoing, but simply to point out that the pursuit is not a pathway flowing with milk and honey, as supposed by some people. Further observations on the remunerative aspect will be given under another heading.

OPERATIVE EQUIPMENT

The three main items of equipment for sound judging are the mind, the eyes and the hands. The function of these three together has already been indicated to aid quick working. They are so great in importance all along the line of action that special mention is made to urge the utmost possible care and protection of them, in order to ensure their full competence in service. Neglect of any of them can bring about doubt and uncertainty in finding the true values of the exhibits.

The mind must be on the immediate job, clear and free from outside interference of any kind and oblivious to the many distractions taking place in close proximity to the judging table. The mind can be controlled to dismiss everything but the rabbits in front of you for assessment. It is not easy perhaps, but it is a worthy acquisition.

Good eyesight is indispensable and should be checked from time to time to make certain that you are seeing things in their right perspective. This applies in particular to colour and shade in colours, and also to slight foreign colours in a colour. To miss the latter fault in the weighing up process can be a disturbing factor to the mind when it is brought to notice (as it surely will be) by someone all set to criticise on the smallest provocation. If such a thing happens it can give an uncomfortable feeling and perhaps upset a normal balance for a time.

The care of the hands ought to be a major concern of every judge. There is little excuse for these to be unkempt, no matter what other work they have to do. The nature of ones everyday occupation may cause wear, tear and soil to the hands. Given, however, sufficient and regular attention, with the aid of one of the many excellent preparations on the market for this special purpose, they may be kept in a reasonable state so that the sense of feel is not impaired; without care they also look unsightly.

One school of thought suggests that it does not matter what the condition of the hands are in if only Fancy breeds claim the judge's attention. It may be true in some ways that the hands are less important when type, style, colour and markings take pre-eminence, but not all fancy breeds rely entirely on visual qualities to complete their excellence.　The Angora is at least one exception.

In the handling of all fur breeds where texture is of great importance, suppleness with surface smoothness should be the aim. It enables the hand to glide through the coat, collecting the evidence relating to that which is being sought. The hands are on view to the onlookers all the time judging is in progress. Their condition must be compatible with that of the best stock under examination. Pride in the state of the hands is the prerogative of the judge. Not for one moment can it be thought ostentatious.

JUDGING PRACTICES

At the very commencement in active work, in fact at the first awakening interest in it, the red herring of judging to Standard will cross your path. The term is in constant use wherever rabbit judging takes place. Its exact meaning is hard, indeed almost impossible, to define to give satisfaction in any argument centering around the expression. In the main it is brought into play to offset disappointment, or dissatisfaction, by someone in disagreement with the result of the judge's findings. It usually relates to one or more minor points, rarely to a major oversight on the part of the person controlling the awards. The best that can be said on the 'judging to standard' bogey is that its a useful spear-head in attack, but there is little excuse to make it and little or no substance to back it.

No judge with experience has use for it as a weapon of defence. All will agree that the standard of a breed is the ideal which has however never been attained by any breeder. It might be thought fair to ask why 'judging to standard' is something forlorn. The previous sentence gives some indication of the answer. If the standards for the breeds receive close scrutiny, and if their specific directions only are applied to actual judging practice, a more complete understanding is possible.

Standards give the maximum points for certain main qualities such as colour, coat, type, markings, condition etc, for the different breeds. They fail to indicate how the judge is to deal with the numerous imperfections found in exhibits. The standard cannot lay down the precise penalty to impose for the irregular line in marking, nor for a missing or misplaced spot from the ideal pattern. Either fault is exposed to fluctuating opinion.

Colour is quoted in general terms, ie. white, black, blue or brown. Think on these. The many shades classified within each colour will perplex as to the implied ideal. When the combination in colours is the order in the standard, the exact proportion one with another is always open to challenge.

Density, length and texture usually have a given number of points to contribute to the grand total making perfection. We can never be certain that the density is complete, the length minutely correct, or the texture superb.

Type may appear to be just about perfect, until a slightly better proportioned specimen arrives to suggest a more pleasing contour. Again, condition in body and coat may alter views when examination passes from one rabbit to another. Who, in all the wide world, can pin point definite exactitude in any one of those things.

Enough has been written to show how incomplete is the 'Standard of Excellence' as a means to decide relative values between competing exhibits which fail to scale up to perfection. Thus the judge is left to interpret the many imperfect characteristics met with from a personal viewpoint. This brings the British Way in rabbit judging to one of 'Comparison', with the standard of excellence of the supreme and important qualities firmly fixed in the mind of the judge.

To the British rabbit Fancy, its system of judging is generally accepted as the most fair and satisfactory way to do justice to both exhibit and exhibitor.

We have in the past heard (and may again in the future hear) voices acclaiming the worth of points judging on the most elaborate basis. The system is that the judge fills in a score card for each exhibit, showing how the animal compares with its standard in every point. The totals give the placings. Before any kind of change from the present method to such a system could take place, the amount of revision needed to transform the standards suitably to cover every contingent (both for credit and debit values) would be colossal. Specified points, to add to or subtract from a grand total, would have to be set out with clarity. In theory such a comprehensive direction seems well nigh infallible, and indeed might be if the individual computations were equitable. We all know the futility in this wishful idea.

No two minds think exactly alike on a rabbit's properties, though more than one person may get the same rabbit to the top of its class on the same day, and other on subsequent occasions while its all round peak condition lasts. It is more than doubtful, however, if any two of several score cards relating to the same rabbit, covering a series of competitive events would tally. The final total of points in each case might vary by 20 and the units adding up to the total might be anything but uniform. All these variations would have the tendency to baffle the owner as to the things in which the rabbit excels or fails.

The points method of judging would need an entire change of procedure from collective comparison judging to single individual assessment of exhibits, and thought will show how chaotic the one by one movement might prove. The single rabbit on its own can appear to be quite good in all respects until a superior one comes along to challenge it. If the judge marks the good rabbit high in points on its score card, and the better one arrives later, there may not be a sufficient number of points left to give full justice to the second. If the judge works 'canny' marking the good rabbit low in points, to avoid possible miscalculations of this nature, and then finds it is the best in class, the position is not improved, as the winning exhibit is graded low. This analogy may seem fantastic to some, but not all judges are good sound mathematicians.

Another important point in this system of judging is that a number of exhibits in a class will have identical numbers of points.

It is difficult to see any advantage in a change from our well tried formula. It has stood the test of time and is suited to our way of conducting shows. The more elaborate points method in making awards may be suitable to other Countries, where shows cover a longer period in time, where judges have a less number of exhibits to deal with, and can wander around from pen to pen, noting the likely candidates for honours, before getting down to the final critique and allocation of points.

To reach the climax in judging any class of rabbits, there must be some recourse to comparison of competitors, otherwise the best might not head the class.

LOYALTIES IN SATISFYING JUDGING

The loyalties in actual judging are at least fourfold. Not one should be lost sight of whenever judging is being carried out. One loyalty is to the B.R.C. rules which are mandatory at most shows. Even if they are not, their set line is paramount in guidance. To observe them fully on every occasion is to safeguard the best interest of everyone.

The Society or Club who have accepted your services to judge is also entitled to unstinting loyalty and co-operation in their plan of action. It must be borne in mind that the best of plans do go astray, however carefully laid by promoters. You will be expected to adapt yourself to unforeseen emergencies, no matter what they be. Acquiesce with graciousness, it will go down to your credit as a pleasing attribute.

There is also the strict duty to your own conscience. Be scrupulous in thought and deed without partiality to animal or person and you will avoid serious recriminations, inward or outward, which disturb peace of mind. This is priceless to self contentment.

Above all there must be sincere consideration given to supporters and their entries. All are equal, from one standpoint, having a mutual stake in the class, by paying the same fee for the opportunity to win or a proportional placing based on fair examination. All this may seem exacting, perhaps formidable, to someone on the threshold of judging appointments, but if you meet these necessary obligations without wavering, they merge together automatically and become natural in inclination, thus leaving concentration clear to work out the degree in quality of the rivals.

CLASS PRESENT AND CORRECT

It may be thought unnecessary to point out the need to make sure that all rabbits placed on the table correspond to the numbers entered in the judging book, and carry the correct ear label of identification. You might think it is the book steward's job to check these things. While most can be relied on to do it thoroughly, faultlessly, it is as well to keep an eye on what is happening. The final responsibility rests on you.

Mistakes often occur when more than one rabbit arrives at the table simultaneously at the start of a new class. Stewards return with their charges needing ear labels, and numbers are called from several directions at the same time. The checker ticks off the arrivals in the book, writes out labels and hands them out. It is in this brief rush where a cross-over in identification marks may take place. It is up to the judge to supervise carefully such a situation, to guard against wrong award recording, re-penning jumbles, and additional fatigues to stewards who have to compare ring numbers with entry forms at the Show Secretary's office, or even hunt through travelling boxes for a number on a label, to rectify the query. All this will waste precious time. When you are certain all is in order numerically, the real business can begin.

HANDLING STOCK

It is obvious that no true appreciation of make up, condition or rank of any rabbit can be made by the judge unless it is handled in examination, and yet complaints are made from time to time on the inadequate handling of exhibits by some judges. The contention of the complainants is that a bad fault may have been missed by the judge not being sufficiently observant.

This may be true in many cases. No judge, whatever his experience or status in the rabbit world, should allow a class entry to go back to its pen from the table without picking it up to look at the underparts. Laxness in this respect allows vent disease and hutch burn to escape detection, white patches and hairs that ought not to be there to get away with it, and even Does to win Buck classes and the reverse.

Many exhibits appear to be in perfect coat condition when looking down at the back and sides, but moult and old coat in evidence may be found when inspection of the under body takes place. This alters the first visionary concept greatly and strengthens the claim for the unseen to be seen before deciding any order in merit.

Handle every rabbit brought to you for your opinion gently but firmly, taking the weight of it in one hand placed under its hind quarters, steadying the animal with the other hand holding the ears. In picking up in this way the first cursory look can after some practice and experience give several simple points which need checking. It can be seen if the rabbit complies with the ringing regulation in as far as wearing a ring goes or the presence of white toe nails in breeds where they are to be penalised, or fore feet free from mucous matting and rubbing, condition of chest fur. It is surprising the number of items that can be taken into account by one glance. It will be fully recognised that there are many breeds, such as Dutch, English, Silvers, Tans etc, that cannot be correctly judged unless lifted clear of the table. It is mainly fur breeds which invite this slackness.

After a preliminary observation is over do not drop the exhibit on to the table with a bump. This may disturb the tranquillity of stock, stewards and viewers. Replace with care is the motto, whatever the opinion arrived at of its quality. If it is poor in your estimation it is still entitled to identical treatment with the best of its company.

Another bad form of handling which is sometimes seen, brings strong resentment from the receiver and awe to the face of watchers, is to drag a rabbit across the table by its ears for close inspection. Its a lazy way of getting what you want, unnecessary and undignified to the office of judge. Above all it sets a bad example to stewards who may be training themselves for a position on your side of the table. If any rabbit is beyond comfortable reach indicate to the attendant the one required and it will be eased towards you to facilitate a clean decent lift more in keeping with the best traditions.

Most Judges use two other forms of handling. The first is usually employed to alter the line in precedence. For this the hand is placed underneath the exhibit to go up or down the scale of merit, the other hand stabilising the balance by the ears. In dealing with the second method, usually for a closer scrutiny of the hindquarters, again place one hand underneath the exhibit leaving the front feet resting on the table while the other hand helps to seek that which is sought. This mode in transportation is quite alright, it brings no discomfort to the rabbit if care is exercised, on the other hand if there is carelessness on the part of the handler both may suffer with the latter coming off worse. Place the fork made by the thumb and index finger underneath the rabbit well back into the rabbits thighs bringing the forearm in a direct line with its body toward the head as is possible so there is little or no pressure on the stomach or intestines. Remember the rabbit if resentful, strikes with the hind feet backwards and slightly outwards, if the forearm is at right angles to its body the liability to receive annoying, if not over serious lacerations to the wrist, is fairly certain. With the hold as mentioned, the kicking movement can be partially checked, the back of the hand acts as a buffer to the upper part of the leg to hamper the first forward impetus to the strike. Use this form in handling judiciously. Never toss a rabbit from position to position by one hand placed under the abdomen. This indicates thoughtless action which no one really intends if there is regard for dumb livestock.

A few breeds, such as Polish and Dwarfs cannot be moved about by the ears. It just is not done. The ears are too small and important to risk damage to the carriage of them. The usual way of lifting these breeds is a light grip over the back, thumb on one side, fingers on the other, just in front of the hind legs and behind the ribs, it presents no difficulty once the art is acquired. Angoras may be lifted by the lower part of the coat to examine feet furnishings and belly, care must be exercised in taking grip on each side to give perfect balance to the weight.

Many judges develop ways distinctive to themselves in handling the various types of stock. Most are worth observing to find out if you can better your workmanship.

All knowledgeable persons connected with rabbits will look askance if one should be grasped by the scruff of its neck or by the skin of the back and allowed to dangle in mid-air. The result of this harsh treatment to short hair breeds is the bruising of the skin tissues at the point of grip. Invariably when this happens the finger pressures reflect as deeper coloured patches at hair tips, within a few days, thereby spoiling the chance of any such rabbit for future show honours for a long time, perhaps for ever. Even a complete moult may fail to repair or reinstate evenness in colour. As a judge you ought not to be guilty of this crime or countenance it in others.

On occasions one is faced with the exhibit who stoutly resists the first approach to the ordeal of close scrutiny, either through fear, lack of training for the mission of show life, or by unfamiliar surroundings. Excitement due to the near proximity of others of its kind opposite in sex is another cause. It can also be bad temper. Whatever the inducement never restrain the wayward struggler by force for damage can be caused by the application of superior strength. Immediately you sense your wishes are opposed put the resenter down and pacify it by gently stroking its forehead just above the eye level and in front of ear base, using a tickling motion with the fore-finger. Turn your attention to another in the class for a short spell. On returning to the opposition member, repeat the finger caress before proceeding with the inspection and you will generally find you have inspired a more willing submissiveness.

Always display the highest standard in sound, careful and considerate handling of each exhibit; it is just as easy in performance as the heedless unconcerned way, and so much more pleasing in effect.

Following on the handling comes the sorting. You must sift these things you have felt, seen and sensed, and get them in their right perspective according to traditional worth. It is expedient that one keeps somewhere within the realm of general all round acceptance with the final pronouncement on the class. Otherwise the air about will become charged with seething dissatisfaction from interested bystanders, giving uncomfortable feelings, and upsetting tranquillity for further proceeding. Nothing daunts self reliance more than this kind of atmosphere or adds to confusion in an early judging career. It has already been intimated how to avoid such embarrassment and it will not arise if the preparation to judge has been built up along sound lines. It is only necessary to apply the dictates of observation, thought and touch, free from interference by any agent, to pass criticism by the same margin as another judge, even if of long standing.

None can evade mild privileged censure when acting in this capacity, it is part and parcel of the appointment.

Some vital conclusions having to be made, centre in colour, coat, type and markings. Not one of these can claim complete conclusiveness in exposition for all are subject to the individual variations in taste. At the same time there is a remarkable closeness in interpretation of these features when they present themselves, at high quality level, to expounders who have learned the job thoroughly. This is the reason why the first class specimens win here, there, everywhere, under all and sundry, and accounts for the worthy Champions made. One secret to success in judging is to be consistent in the basic things of first priority in as much as they are presented well up to standard for judgement.

COLOUR

Down through the known history of rabbit keeping colour has been a main topic of discussion. What the right shade is, in one person's mind and eye, is a wee bit out in anothers. The exactness visualised by someone if reproduced on to a colour card, will not meet mutual approval for this very reason. To compare colours of the same given descriptive name but with different origins in manufacture only adds to indecision in proclaiming the ideal, for no two will be perfect in match. It is said the 'Black' has many shades, each being distinct and recognisable to the expert Colourman, but there is no universal declared perfection in any shade as being the only true black.

This same state can be applied to the whole range of colours. With so many close resemblances to choose from, contending for rightness, it is no small wonder that uniform consistency fails to take place in colour interpretation, even by judges who are supposed to point the way in it.

With one or two rabbit colours we are soundly directed as to what is preferable. In white, the stress is often laid on 'Pure'. A creamy or dirty shade is not then desirable. One ought not to stray with such a directive for most can discern the cleanest white. In black, the operative word is 'Sound' or 'Jet'. Precision in meaning here is not hard to understand in spite of the earlier statement on its many degrees in density.

Blue, is not an easy colour to deal with in that the prefix to it may be dark, deep, slate, medium, light, lavender or smoke, all of which are intended to help in the separation of shade. The difficulty is to know where one starts and ends; it is the personal calculation that has to decide. Brown, in rich dark chocolate, Chestnut, medium, sepia, beaver, brown-grey, are no less a problem to separate. Greys, Lilac, Tortoiseshell, Orange, Fawn, and others, with which mixtures of this, that and the other have to be dealt.

It is doubtful if a Solomon could transcribe accurate enlightenment, beneficial to students of the colour controversy. It is a subject in which we may all beg to slightly differ. All that can be said to help confidence in selection from a choice is that where the given colour is preceded by, deep, dark, dense, take it down to its maximum depth, i.e. blue and brown to border black, but still clearly perceptible from it. In all other shades, blends and combinations work out your own conception from what is seen as general acceptance centering around the usual argumentative circle. So long as a judge keeps within the narrow limit of any given hue, there must be tolerance with the preferrer on the part of others who see it with trifling difference. Stick always to the near ideal that convinces you, and you have given the cue to exhibitors of your personal concept in this controversial subject on colour. It is in this way that all Judges establish their likes, dislikes and leanings, for this or that particular shade throughout the fancy to be registered by all whom it may concern.

EFFECTS OF LIGHT

The condition of the prevailing light may be a source of trouble to the judge's conception of any colour. It can be the greatest enemy and deceiver to him. If the light is good then all is well, there will be no undue worry for the true reflection will transmit correctly to mind the colour soundness or deficiency. The frequent dull weather met with during late autumn and winter brings to the judge some small sense of being at a disadvantage to determine colour with absolute surety. The poorly lit Hall gives the same feeling.

Subdued light, whatever the cause, does favour the dark self colours, in that some unwanted shade, (such as a rusty tinge in black, a gingery tint in brown and blue, or odd white hairs in either), may pass detection. No one likes to miss this kind of blemish but there is some excuse for it under bad light conditions.

The reaction in dealing with light colours, (Lilac, Lavender Blue, Pearl, Fawn, lightish top colour mixtures) and breeds with side shading, in a poor light is the opposite and is to their disadvantage, for it robs the delicate colour of its delicacy and brilliance. Exercise extra care when sorting this section in such unfavourable conditions, otherwise one is apt to lose sight of the full beauty of light coloured exhibits, thereby under-rating them.

The kind of light most tantalising, annoying and aggravating is the alternating one. It is the work of nature and outside human control. Scudding cloud passing the sun is one great offender, casting shadows from all angles at a crucial moment when you are trying to separate a deciding issue on colour. Two rabbits, seemingly equal in this feature, can, in a quick changing light give one a real headache in arriving at the right solution. At one moment you are certain as to the better, in a flash the focus transfers to the other giving that the lead. This process will repeat itself again and again with a rapidity that confuses the mind. In a really tight finish between two exhibits this situation is baffling to any judge and its then a case of using every grain of patience to wait for a sufficient period of constant light to determine which is to win.

When working under canvas be careful in the position selected for the judging table. Marquee roof sections are habitually contrasting in transparency. Some are drab in the extreme, others are just drab, none being crystal clear to allow free passage to light. Get beneath the most free from obstruction, and shun the site set under overhead divisions unequal in clearness. Its the even downward shaft of light one wants to make the environment identical for all competitors.

ARTIFICIAL LIGHT

This is not a full substitute for the average good daylight but it is steady. Eyesight will adjust itself to this form of illumination to give reasonable assurance in colour estimation which will obviate wide diversion from the natural bloom carried by the rabbit. It is in fact a good compromise between the worst and the best natural light, though making the judges' task a bit more tiring by added penetration. Fluorescent light in any form is an enemy indeed, it breaks down all richness and lustre so much that the colour seen appears totally different from the actual colour known to be there.

One golden rule to observe, whatever the light problem, is to consider the colour value of each exhibit at near enough the same area of the judging table.   Choose the part where interference by movement of persons does not cross the line of vision.   Keeping to the one spot cuts the risk of optical inconsistency to a minimum. Never remove one rabbit to another part of the building or take it outside for a closer colour examination, it may favour or disfavour the one and is injustice to all other contenders. Keep the entire class to the same plane for inspection.

There is no cause for alarm when faced with the light handicaps outlined, it is not so serious when judging a class all of the same classified colour. Taking only this one factor into account it will be found that the order in placing would be no different if made in first grade light.

The law in colour comparison works just the same from any given starting point, the best reflects as the best, no matter what the degree of natural or artificial light, so long as colours are not mixed.   But to judge a mixed colour class in dimmed light is a hazard most judges do not cherish in thought, let alone in deed. Fortunately there are other aids to judging unaffected by bad light, to which the experienced judge may resort with safety.

COAT

The importance of different coat properties varies according to the breed and its status. In the majority of Fancy rabbits the chief concern in investigation is for correct textures and lengths. Good, full, short and fine, are the terms in general use to describe what is required with little indication as to the amount.   Where no definite points are allocated to coat in the standard for the breed, the inference is that coat is secondary in importance to other qualities.

Harlequins, Polish, Silvers are moderate exceptions to this general rule, while the Angora is the greatest exception. Coat to the Angora is everything, so much so it seems out of place in the fancy section and yet the coat of sound commercial value is the 'crowning glory' in exhibition.

Density, fullness, length and texture are the basic ingredients to be covered in dealing with coat in all classified Fur breeds. It may be thought that density and fullness are one and the same thing, but density can be present without complete fullness. Many fur rabbits have density from base of rump up over haunches to near the shoulders then it considerably lessens. Full density carries right through to nape of neck.

The sense of touch plays a large part in being accurate in deciding density, but reliance on it alone can let one down.

The oft included clause in many standards 'density to rank above length' gives the clue to a possible misconception that may take place. A lengthy coat, less dense than a shorter one, can give an impression of equal, perhaps more, wealth of coat, to the feeling hand. Six hairs one and a half inches in length measure in bulk that of nine one inch long. Multiply the numbers given by any unit and the illustration takes the same shape. Either coat will fill the hand to the same appreciation but the short hairs need more base area to accommodate them and should take precedence.

Density is the number of hairs packed in a given area. To be quite certain of assessing density the hand and eye must work together. With the hand travelling through the coat observe with the eye the width of clear skin at the hair roots. The wideness, much or little, denotes which is the best coat.

Coat textures vary according to breed. We are advised to

discriminate in terms of, soft, fine, silky and harsh, with some linkage in either two of the first three. Reaction to prescribed substance is purely individual in conception, with fair agreement reigning among the experienced judges as to what constitutes one or the other. The hand again plays the role as detector in finding out how near the ideal is the actual texture. Earlier reference on care of hands is brought again into prominence here. Their condition is important in interpreting the right constitution.

Warning is given that with few exceptions, woolliness in all normal and rex coats is a definite fault to be penalised. This failing creeps into many of the Fur breeds and too often receives the reverse of what its entitled to; commendation instead of condemnation. There ought not to be an atom of doubt in detecting the unwanted woolly coat, this condition is to be easily seen and felt. When present in normal fur there is no gentle resistance to the hand. The coat is listless and lifeless and can be pushed to any position where it stays put. Matting is often at the lower rump due to inter-twining of the undercoat. The face of a rabbit with a woolly textured coat has a 'bushy' look about it instead of being sleek and trim. The near correct texture of the normal coat returns gently to the exact place from where it was disturbed.

The woolly Rex coat presents to the eye an uneven, untidy, unfinished appearance; the hairs curve, curl and twist, in all directions immediately below the top surface. It feels heavy, lumpy and cloggy, hampering the clean clear passage of the hand through it. Fleecy in texture is a fitting description to this class of coat. The fur should stand uprightish to the body giving a smooth, level, surface finish which allows the gentle flowing action over the coat in the test for texture.

In one fur breed only, the New Zealand Red, is harshness

in texture called for. This condition in coat is easy to understand and feel, it is the contrast to the generality in other fur breeds, rather springy to the touch.

TYPE

Type, shape or style is the overall cut-line of the rabbit. Each breed has its own graceful curves and deportment with some in close resemblance to each other.

Ear length and setting is usually proportionate to size and weight. Lengthy ears on the small or medium breeds upset balance, while small neat ears on a large breed are out of keeping with the overall symmetrical ratio. The one exception to relative proportion in this instance is of course the English Lop, where ear length, width, shape, substance and carriage, account for half the total amount of points allocated to the typical specimen. It is thought not to be out of place here to interject a warning concerning the one time 'King of the Fancy'. Haphazard and incorrect method in ear measurement is a real source of annoyance to all who have regard for the Lop. The length must be beneath the ears, gently stretching to the full extent. To measure width, fold the ear at its maximum breadth to get a straight cross line. Use only a rigid measuring rule, or the given inches will be open to challenge. Carry your own equipment for this purpose to save being 'caught out' when the occasional Lop comes along to you for examination and judgement. The 3 foot folding wooden rule is suitable, it is easy to carry, fitting into a small space. The yard tape is useless, and the thin steel roll type is difficult to manipulate to obtain accuracy owing to its tendency to whip and bend. [Note: When this book was written the only lop in the country was the English Lop. Lops have now become very popular and there are a number of different lop breeds. Dwarf

Lops have particularly increased in numbers as have also Cashmere Lops, and French, German and Meissner Lops].

Cobby, inclined to cobbiness, long in body, racy, mandolin, snaky, all these refer to type, with which judges must become familiar, so as to apply each appropriately in the rightful manner due to the breed as part of its make up.

The Chinchilla and the Chinchilla Giganta provide a suitable example of the cardinal points both being of similar colouration but well removed in type. The Chinchilla should be moderate in length of body, with small and erect ears, fine in bone. The Giganta should be long and graceful in body, with ears and limbs in proportion to its size. The weight difference between the two is almost double. The former indicates the neat compact pattern, the latter calls for a sturdy, robust, heavy build. The contrast in shape is most marked when one of each, near correct in proportion is placed side by side. The rabbit over stepping the Chin limits and not up to Giganta dimensions, however good in coat or colour is neither one or the other, for it fails to conform to either type as depicted in the respective standards.

To observe the silhouette of any breed satisfactorily, turn the rabbit broad side on to view, stand back a couple of paces and you will then see the real formation correctly. The best proportioning is made at a slight distance from the rabbit. Is the head snipey ? Poor in size and shape in relation to the body? Is the neck long or scraggy ? The top body line flat when it ought to be arched? Is the rump chopped or square instead of continuing in a gradual curve? These and other points relative to type have to be given fair consideration. The major faults to mar breed style should not escape the notice of a judge. In making sure they are non-existent, minor ones may be noted to help separate close rivals.

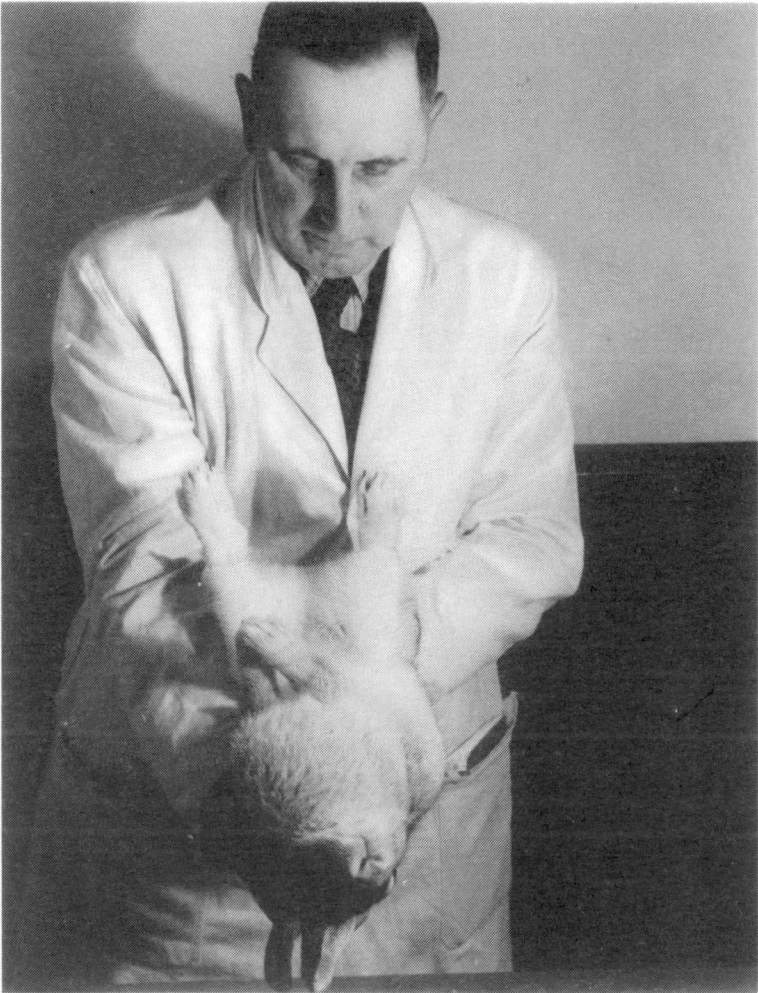

The Author taking a general look under

Steadying on the table

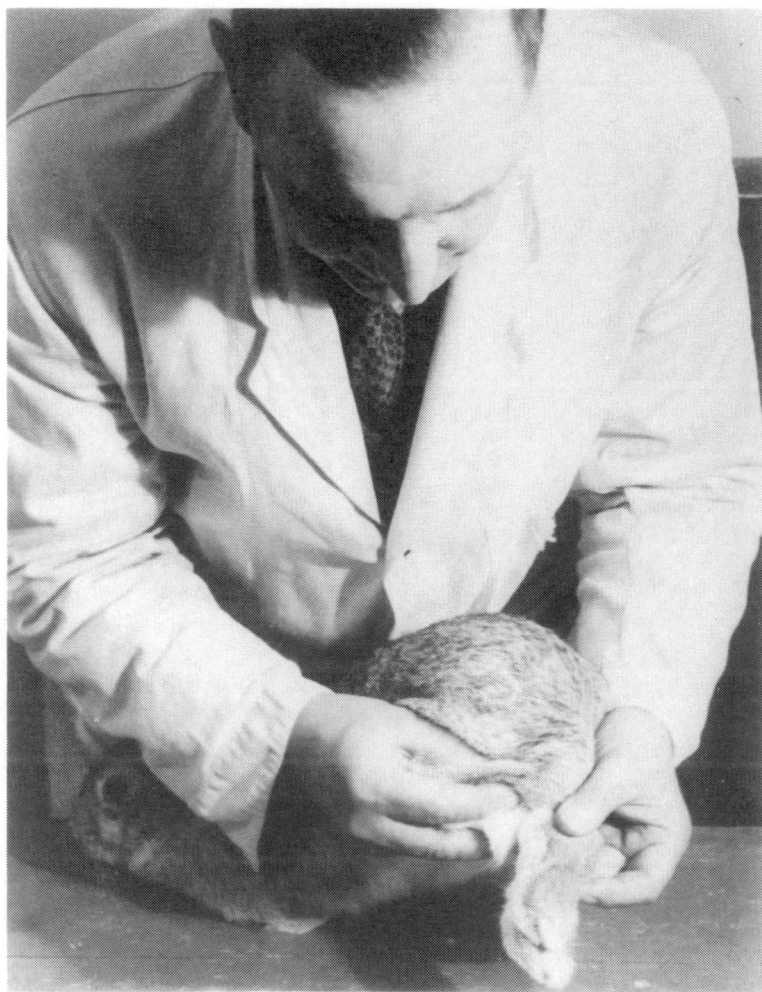

Checking the ring number

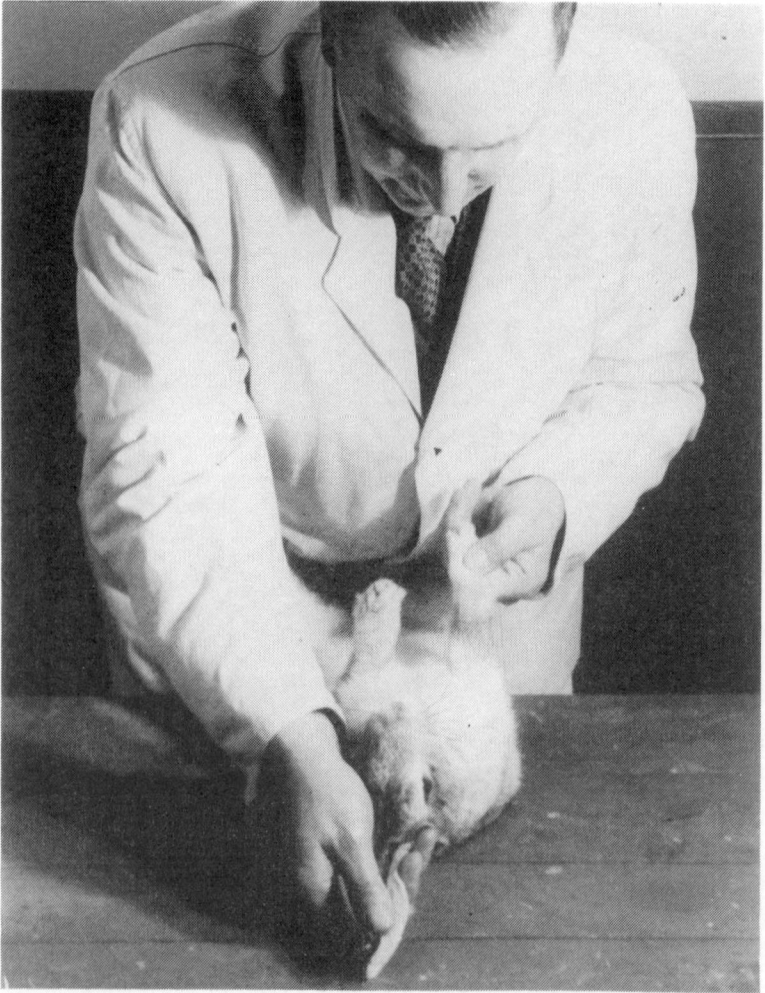

Checking forefeet at the judging table

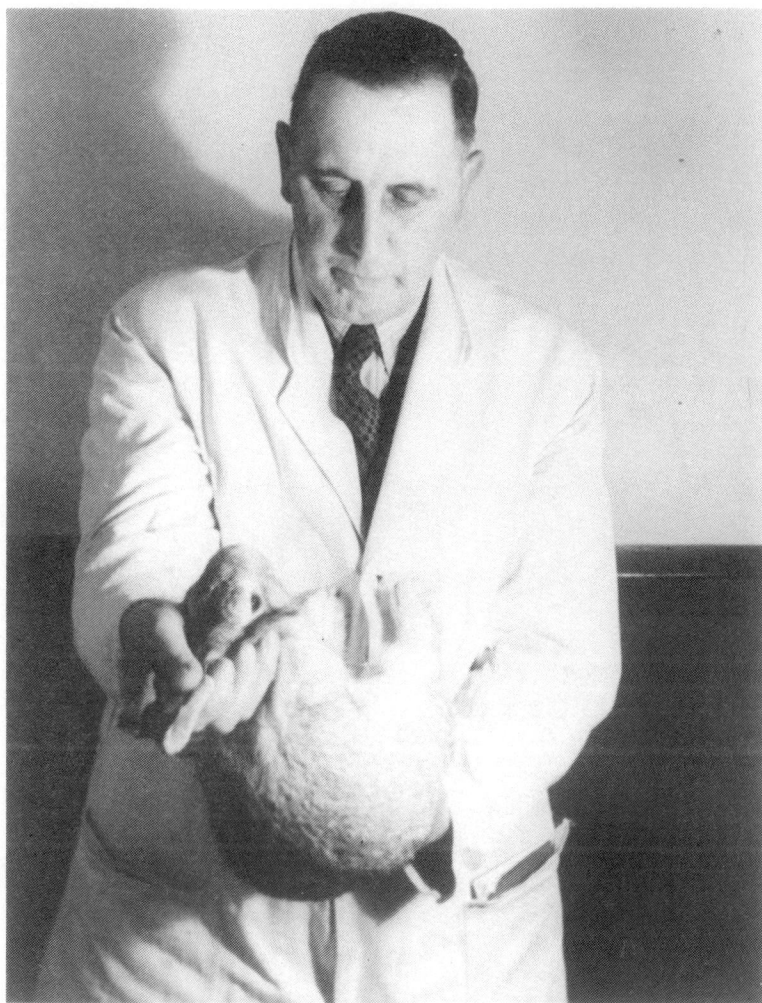

The Author taking a general look at the chest and under

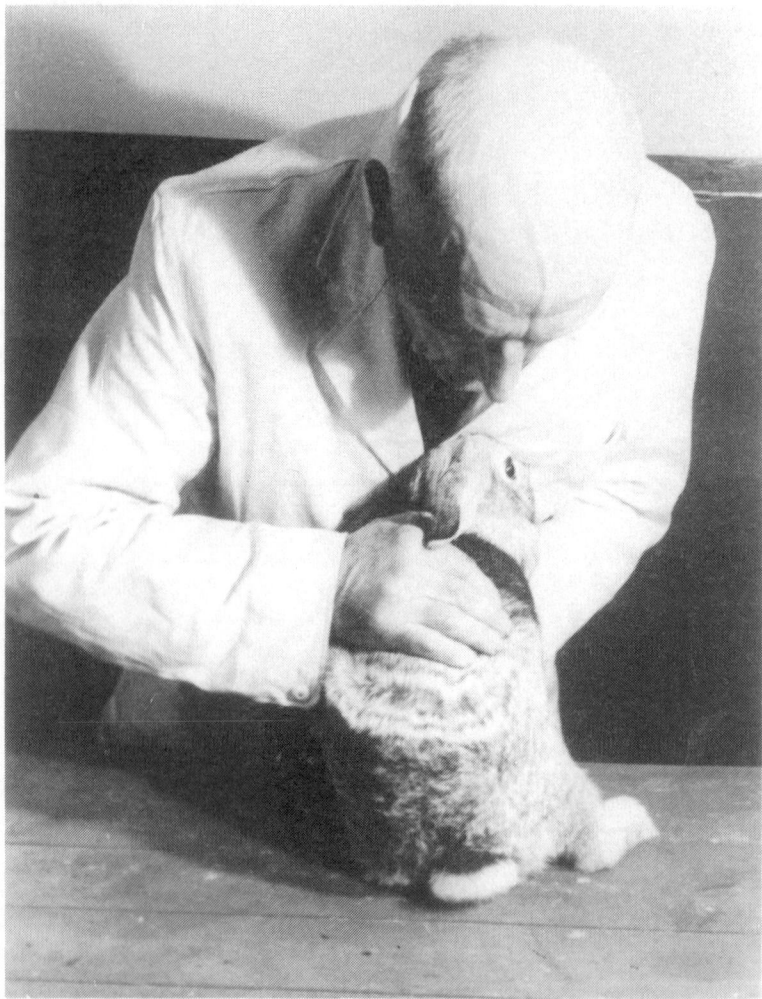

Thomas Leaver
The original judging teacher of Harold Dowle

Harold Dowle in the Royal Flying Corps

The Author at the judging table
with F.G. Woodgate (left) and C. Dickens (right)

Harold Dowle outside his rabbitry

CONDITION

There appears to be a partial mystery attached to the value of this essential in exhibition. Some standards fail to mention it specifically, others tie it up with something else; those making a feature of it allocate very few points of the grand total to it.

The enquiry is not rare 'why so little for so much' when prime condition of body and coat, constitutes the first essential of keen Showmanship. We can only conclude that it must be taken as an automatic prelude to the act of showing if a measure of success is expected.

Many a judge, past and present, has extolled the fact that a rabbit in first class condition carrying its other breed qualities is already more than half-way to the top of its class. Judges revel in handling stock in superb fitness, it always commands that second look, while the rabbit out of form is apt to get short consideration with quick dismissal. The rabbit low in flesh covering will be boney and angular in appearance. In this state, belly size seems out of proportion to the remainder of its body. It will also reflect on type, already dealt with. Fullness, firmness and hardness in flesh cannot altogether replace defective shape, but it adds up to give maximum support to the natural structure.

In dissecting these simple characteristics from the rabbit's complete make up, partiality to one or the other must be avoided at all cost. No one thing, however outstanding by itself, can make the ideal class leader. Near perfect marking in a marked breed, if it lacks colour, type or condition, cannot claim the over-riding position. Preferences should go to the rabbit a little behind in markings with better supporting factors. Coat minus good sound colour, and the reverse, in fur breeds, miss the mark of distinction. Often the commercial value of the pelt, highly sought after in furriery, blinds the judge to other shortcomings in a particular exhibit.   Whatever the designation of a breed, immediately it is entered in competition with others of its kind for honours, it becomes an exhibition specimen of its breed.   It cannot afford to be good only in part. It must offer the all round characteristics as prescribed in its standard of excellence to qualify for high rewards on the show bench.

FIXED AND OBSCURE PENALTIES FOR FAULTS

Out and out faults to warrant disqualification are not widely advertised in general breed standards. Some standards do give clear cut guidance on a number of disqualifications, others stop short with just one or two examples, while we have a few which do not even mention the penalty.   Where the actual disqualification is mentioned, the judge is free from dilemma. There is no option but to dismiss the offender from competition. White patches, Putty Nose, Drooping Ears, Specked, odd or wrong coloured eyes, Crooked legs, Ill health, any form of disease. This collection of faults and ills, compiled from a wide range of standards cover the main issues calling for extreme action. Any of these may be found in a rabbit of any breed from time to time. In spite of no reference to one or the other fault in its standard, the rabbit should be sent off if one of these general faults is present

No judge can countenance any of the defects as outlined, on the ground of its omission from a breed's standing guide, for all are seriously detrimental to the well-being of the rabbit deserving Show status.

Artificial practices such as trimming, application of colouring matter or over preparation for exhibition, all call for the stern way of elimination when detected. Very little help can be given on this complex question as helpful to the judge gaining early experience. The judge acting against this kind of malpractice with severity, must be absolutely sure of the fact, with cast iron proof to uphold the inditement. To disqualify under the 'irregular preparation' is to accuse someone of downright dishonesty and it must be substantiated if you are to escape possible consequential action. On the other hand, if you are fully convinced a rabbit is not as nature intended it to be, but has received aid to improvement by human agency, you must report the matter, after disqualifying, as directed in B.R.C. rules. Otherwise you fail in your duty, being party to the connivance, by allowing the attempt to cheat to pass. To ignore the rabbit tampered with for the purpose of deception to higher award, by just passing it back to its pen, is not exemplary judging. Shirking responsibility in this way rarely passes un-noticed, if kept up.

In time it will react unfavourably on your reputation. Doubt will arise at sometime in connection with the more natural causes for castaway decisions as to the degree of unfitness or the stage in development of defect. 'Is it bad enough to disqualify?' may come to your mind. Sympathetic leaning to imperfections cannot enter the region of judging.

Most judges can appreciate the resentment of an exhibitor owning an exhibit which is a border line case of pure physical weakness which is disqualified. An exhibitor for example having an excellent rabbit in every respect, with the exception of its legs which are bowed or bandy. Arguments for and against such a rabbit's inclusion in the prize list is often keen. This is curious when, if the lower part of the fore feet turn outward in a marked manner, [splay footed], bone malformation is accepted without quibble. Inward or outward, either condition violates construction of legs. They are to be straight in all breeds. The rabbit has four legs and the judge needs to pay attention to the hind as well as the forelegs on this question of alignment.

Cow hocked or knocked-kneed legs confront you at times. The top part of the leg is tucked away under the culprit, giving a tapering effect to the hind quarters. The hock protruding from its joint at an angle of up to 90 degrees, instead of being parallel with the outside line of the body. This is bone trouble equal to that brought to notice on front feet in some standards and it should not be tolerated.

The drooping or pendant ear needs little explanation. Instead of being upright, it lops down over the face. This chronic ear condition is distinct from weak ear carriage in which ears having a slight list to 'Port or Starboard', being just off the upright. This is a fault not subject to disqualification.

The sneezing rabbit can make you ponder, 'Is it ill-health?' or a passing irritation to which all living humans and animals are susceptible. 'Is it the beginning of a snuffly cold ?', one of the rabbits worst enemy, with the possible risk of infection to others in its company. If the sneeze produces mucous, or excess moisture, your course is obvious. The judge will examine the isolated sneeze closely for any sign of dampness at the nostrils, if found to be dry, the incident is closed, and the exhibit allowed to remain in competition.

Ill-health, any form of disease or deformity covers a very wide field. When any such condition exists it must be severely penalised to prevent encouragement of anything but superb fitness in exhibits. To generalise on the attitude of leading judges toward definite signs of any thing pertaining to ill-health, one could say that the penalty is swift Veto. The best interests of the fancy are served by out-right rejection of this unwanted trend.

It should not be lost sight of that several exhibits classified as 'Outcasts' from breed classes, may be entered in 'Utility Pure Breed' and 'Live Pelt Classes'. Wrong or odd colour eyes, drooping ear, crooked leg, would not impair the commercial or utilitarian value of the exhibit, if other essentials were of high grade. Thus, for serious faults, exhibits 'Go to the wall'. Appeasement ought not to be entertained on any account by awarding the last card of the class to a rabbit of little value. To 'Highly Commend' or 'Commend' as a matter of course, is an infringement to the moral law of judging.

LESSER FAULTS AND FAILINGS

We have numerous little defects in show stock for which there is no set penalty for the judge to impose, they are left to individual discretion. The slight irregularity in a pattern where the dividing line should be clean cut; the missing spot or one out of place; white hairs in a colour fur; white ticks in ears that ought to be clear; the frosted nose with that tantalising bar of light greyish hairs on the nose, carried chiefly by the tan pattern fur breeds; white hairs coming up over the fore toes and white toe nails are all examples.

Going to the opposite end of the rabbit there is the question of tails. Little notice seems to be taken of this appendage by judges, with the possible exception of one or two breeds where the tail carried out of line with the back bone is listed as a fault. It is notable how many of the fur breeds have defective scuts. Some have merely an apology for this, just a stump. Others, no more than half the length it should be. White tipped tails are liable to escape observation on the light colours. There's a host of these little things to be on watch for. They all tax the judge's own initiative in assessment of value in relation to other virtues.

The rabbit free from any small short-coming is still the dream of fanciers. The pattern of the marked breeds lends itself to suggestion for improvement or better balance somewhere. Colour can never be accepted by all as just right. Density in coat is never so full as to leave no room for more hairs to come through. All compositions counting up to the grand total of complete perfection in a breed are subject to this kind of deduction. If it were not so, standards would be obsolete as a formula to judging. The full aggregate in points will always remain elusive to act as a spur to better breeding and retention of interest in exhibition.

This may be a hard fact to accept, when we review the splendid breed Champions, past and present. Judges declare they can deduct points from the best specimen breeders may bring along for their opinion, with full regard to the oft read comment in Show reports 'Hard to fault'. The truth in this reasoning can only be admitted as sound, if the examples quoted are given due consideration. It all depends on the judge's outlook to these failings. Best marking as against the better colour, coat before colour, lengthy coat in front of short and more dense, and so on. Reverse the orders, they will still fit in with someone's preference who officiates. Thus we have a mild clash in assessing the varied minor characteristics of quality. The margin in favour displayed between one exhibit and another may be no more than sufficient to give the separating edge to close rivals, one way or the other, according to the impulse of the person in charge of decision.

These little variations in Judges appraisement, in themselves are not serious enough to confuse from main quality characters. They do account for raising or dropping of exhibits from the higher to immediately lower positions and vice-versa, when subject to diverse opinion. Two capable Judges, handling the same stock in different sections at a Show, may change round each other's leading rabbits within the top half awards, on personal minute examination. There are many, many, known instances to support this statement of almost consistent judging, quite free from connivance. It gives high credit to the general competence of judges to be so near in agreement on merit. This sort of nearness adds a thrilling excitement to expectant exhibitors, most seem to thoroughly enjoy the wee uncertainty it creates, as the final winner is not just a foregone conclusion. The right proportional adjustment to place on minor defects as effecting keen competition is the judge's own prerogative.

When faced with one of the many such minor defects, give it unbiased, thoughtful consideration; balance the pros and cons, then act as honest conviction dictates, in the light of your knowledge. This is the only way to deal with un-classified minor faults.

DISTINGUISHING FEATURES

There is no point in attempting to hide the fact that judges do very often recognise high class rabbits after they have once examined them. The judge's training, by regular constant working experience, makes for a good memory, with keen observation of petty detail. Judges also exchange confidences during their off duty time together, (often when travelling to and from engagements,) so that the little oddities attached to this or that winner goes round and round. therefore it's not surprising that the 'well wearing' exhibit does become familiar, as it travels from show to show. Remember the already stressed opinion that no rabbit of any breed is perfect. It is this situation that may give the clue to a recent introduction, actual or informed. There may be a peculiarity in the pattern in marked breeds; the run in or one colour on to another at some unobtrusive point; one white toe nail when all should be of a specified colour; or the ever so slight nick in an ear. Mannerism in stance when about to be picked up or even a spiteful resentment to handling can produce the same evidence. Many more singular things serve to bring realisation of 'we've met before' or 'yes, so and so has told me all about this blemish or trait'.

All judges have to square up to this 'I know you' situation from time to time and it is a direct challenge to integrity. It can only be dealt with in the strictest sense of the calling ie., fair and just application of the principals expected from you.

Never allow a past reputation of the exhibit to influence proceedings, nor penalise it for any previous judgement, on the basis of 'It's another's turn to win this time'. The only course to adopt is to treat each judging engagement as a complete single unit. The past is gone and finished with, your concern is the immediate present. Train yourself from the beginning to this line in action. It will avoid stray thoughts which breaks down concentration. Disregard the seeming pointer to recognition and your conscience will never be troubled by a mistaken identity - even rabbits have their almost double in appearance. Keep to straight forward judging always, leave all former show results to take care of themselves. Then the best exhibit will come out on top, with the rest following on in order of merit, according to your estimated values. Impartiality to breed, breeder and signs, is one keynote in exemplary judging. By it, you'll gain lasting respect from all who cherish sincerity of purpose in judging.

JUDGES NOTES

These two words appear on each page of all regulation judging books. Convenient space for remarks is left opposite the exhibit's pen number. If the significance attached to this provision is realised and put to use by the judge when all straight classes are judged, valuable data is on record for later reference. Few judges, if any can carry in mind, a complete card index type of remembrance for every rabbit dealt with throughout the average open show. Nevertheless it's surprising how often one needs to regain visual recollection of a rabbit judged, carded or discarded in its class, for a variety of reasons. After all awards have been made and the judge is relaxed from the official role, questions concerning any rabbit coming under jurisdiction are liable to be asked by someone present. It's of little use having the individual brought from the pen to give your reason why it only gained a V.H.C., or no award at all, as it would be outside the surroundings of the original estimation, based on comparison with others in the same category. The re-examination of an exhibit in this manner may cause you to wonder why it failed to do better, as the isolate rabbit may appear to be reasonably good. To be uncertain why the exhibit was placed as it was, makes it difficult to give a convincing verbal reply to the enquirer. The vague answer is as good as no answer.

Further, there is the possible postal enquiry, a few days hence, along the same line. All you can do, if you've nothing to prompt memory, is to be non-committal or frankly admit you can offer no comment. This kind of request is not rare. Many are received on behalf of winners and non-winners alike. Practically all judges accept this additional service as part of their obligation

to the fancy. If it is to be beneficial in enlightenment as to the
faults or failings or qualities of the particular exhibit and helpful to
its owner, then the report passed back must be genuine in
content. The policy of making brief notes on each exhibit will
obviate embarrassment in any way when information is sought
after the actual sorting out has taken place.

The effort expended to have such detail at hand need not
be great, neither need it trespass on time sufficiently to slow down
normal judging progress. Shorthand writing is the ideal for noting
essential features speedily, but not many judges are expert in this
art. All judges should however be quite capable of working out a
set of abbreviations as a substitute, seeing that the range of
words to portray the good, moderate or poor specimen is not
great. Colour may be cut to 'clr', with a prefix such as 'gd' for
good, 'fr' if not so good, only fair, 'pr' if poor. 'sz' will indicate size,
'dty' density, 'typ' type. 'lks' will do for something lacking, 'fls'
does for a failing somewhere. These few illustrations will show
the idea to work out and fix in mind. Once you have devised such
a system, in a short time it will be become automatic in operation.
A glance back to the notes made will bring a clear image of the
exhibit to the fore and all you wish to know of it.

DUPLICATE CLASS JUDGING

Duplication is no doubt the Show Secretary's delight. It
adds to the income, with little additional expense, time and
trouble, over the single entry. Duplicate entries are indeed a
boon to all shows. To the judge however, extensive duplicate
entries mean complication, for the sequence in competitors
change with each succeeding class. One number goes out,
another comes in. Sometimes a complete new set take the table,

to be followed by a combination from duplicates already judged. The strong Breeders or Challenge class may have in it more straight breed winners than the number of cards allocated for distribution. When this happens care must be taken to ensure the claims of the good 2nd or 3rd are not forgotten, some 1sts may head a mediocre collection. [Note. Now in 1992 the block entry system is more usual which makes the challenge classes easier - except of course 'Breeder's', 'Bucks', 'Ladies' and others.]

With unlimited criss-crossing of exhibits in this kind of competition it is only to be expected that the judge has to refer back to previous classes to keep the order in succession right and to eliminate entrants having no chance of a place in the cards. It does away with unnecessary handling of stock and saves the stewards needless steps.

This form of book judging is on occasions strongly criticised. But, provided the check back is thorough and your comments against any rabbit concerned taken into just account, then its perfectly fair. The rabbit placed 2nd in its straight breed class gains a commended card in a duplicate class, if it can only still hold 7th place in the following duplication, why bring out the rabbit 3rd to it in its first class, if entered against it here.

The chief danger in resorting to book reference come with the first of the duplicate classes. If you allow straight breed class position to override fair judgement and do not give consideration due to all claimants, (some of which may have had a hard struggle to get their mid class place because of outstanding level quality in opposition) then you will invite murmurs of discontent. To admit - if there's enough eligible - only class leaders in these additional classes, is far from being circumspect. Any protest against this rather easy way out is legitimate. It is not unique to find 3rds better in substance for their breed, than some 1sts of another, even V.H.C.s, more desirable than 3rds, and so on, when the issue is taken in dead earnest.

Having once balanced individual exhibits, one with another to fix precedence in merit, most following combinations can be judged with the minimum number of rabbits on the table and back checking. All duplicate classes are the climax to higher awards and trophies. If an aspirant has been beaten in preliminary competition leading up to these finals, by others still competing, then by rights, it has no chance to succeed, either by its absence from or presence at the table.

The rule met with here and there, that every rabbit duplicated into - whatever the class might be - must come out for further inspection is nothing more than formality, and waste of time and effort. Audible thoughts expressed at times on this manner in judging hint at precautionary measures in operation, to avoid crossing awards. While there may be some small truth in this way of thinking, its a precaution that harms no one. It is up to every judge to see that no major blunder is made at this stage in the position of awards. If such a blunder occurs it will be a delight to some exhibitors and an annoyance to others.

Judges are entitled to safeguard themselves from this happening by the means at their disposal ie., the judging book, which gives a true recording of their logical conclusions when conditions were most favourable to determine the best from the rest. Judging amenities deteriorate, more often than not when duplication classes come on towards the end of the day and thus slightly distort the actual qualities. The original deductions arrived at in values must follow on through the series, to make intelligent understanding. To take advantage of possessed information relative to the proceeding, is justifiable.

AGE LIMIT CLASSES

It matters not if the age limit class be under 13 weeks, 4, 5 or 6 months, either will tax the judge's power in discrimination as to the legitimacy of some exhibit entered therein. We are all well acquainted with the fate in store for the rabbit overstepping the boundary line in any restricted age class. The judge in a tactful way marks O.D. (over developed) or T.D. (too developed) opposite its pen number in the judging book and it goes to 'Coventry' in disgrace. It can only then be brought back into competition, if entered in a following Any Age or year bred class.

Whatever the term used to denote disqualification for the transgression, the stigma of 'believed over age' is implied. It may be thought futile to make reference to this complex question, for which there is no known reliable way to substantiate the right of inclusion or exclusion of a suspect. Nevertheless the situation confronts the judge continually whenever young classes are included in the schedule.

With due regard to insolubility, no direct solution to the problem is offered in the following observations. The intention is to help young judges in their early experience, to weigh up carefully, some things that can deceive calculation on supposed date of birth, before rejecting outright the doubtful entry. The older judge with plenty of show experience is well versed in the correct approach to what is one of the more difficult decisions to reach.

Everyone connected with show business understands the main objects in providing under certain age classes. They are for the specific purpose of exhibiting immature rabbits having potential qualities indicative of first rate quality when mature. Taking the under 5 months class, catering for youngsters of the medium size breeds, the judge expects to handle rabbits still showing signs of intermediate development. Unfinished in coat perfection, proportionate in frame and weight to the adult standard, carrying the genuine looks of a growing rabbit with it. It is the rabbit which is nearly finished in coat, very well grown, firm in flesh and decidedly more forward in appearance to its class mates, with a young adult look about it, that starts 'eyebrows to raise' and suspicion to enter the mind. At once the search is on to find something to convince that it has had longer life than inferred in class terminology.

Before going on to generalities that are supposed to support believed violation of the restriction, one important point should not be overlooked. Some allowance must be made by the judge for the proficiency and skill of the breeder-exhibitor. Outstanding stock raisers, who by strict attention to feeding, hygiene, growth inducements and all supplements to rapid maturity, should not be penalised for achieved result in effort, which puts a 'plus' on the rabbit, making it above the average for its age. The slightly forced type of youngster is able to pass the usual examination test, claws, flesh solidity, sexual organs. The claws will be moderately fine in substance, fairly sharp at points, practically hidden by the toe fur. Flesh is supple to the feel with little trace of muscular tissue. The male sex organs will vary but should not be too prominent, in the female it will be pale in colour, narrow in outline.

There is one other quite popular sign seized on as a guide to action in this matter. This is a patch of dead hairs on the forehead which may be from the nest or intermediate coat. To some judges it is the 'all clear' to admittance, but this symbol has little reliance as to age; it may be found at all times, on many rabbits, right up to the final adult coat moult. Teeth examination: 'Has this any discernible relation to relative age'? While no authenticity is claimed in the opinion expressed there are grounds to believe that a parallel exists. The two lower teeth of the younger rabbit are bright and white, with no space to be seen between them, slightly tapering at the top edge. With natural growth and normal use, a marked change can be detected at the 5-6 month stage. They become dull in colour, broaden at the top and spread, to give a distinct clearance at the highest point. To state the exact age when the parting is evident would be presumptuous, but there is good reason to think it is obscure up to about the fifth month. This passage has been written with some reluctance owing to lack of known reliable research into its possible connection. There is also the danger that this theory is derived from a string of coincidences. It needs more than one small rabbitry's production to confirm (with any degree of certainty) the feasibility of entertaining this means as a more clear guide to the perplexity.

The idea has been passed to other busy judges with the hope that something more tangible may emerge to tie up with other measures in common use by them at shows, to reassure the right to disqualify or not. In any case this mode of determination is no more haphazard than the other suppositions employed.

Over Developed, Over Age, name it as you will, is chiefly the judge's prerogative. It is up to all who accept the office seriously, to probe into every indication that will help close the gap of uncertain, un-systematic administration in this one thing. It can be seen by the brief descriptions given where and how judges draw their inference to admit or cast out exhibits from age limit classes, though we cannot pin point decisiveness in either. The Judge, hardened in service, works to an instinctive line of demarcation in age build up. The line is clearly impressed on the mind and is very real to the individual concerned. It is by this line that all deductions to age acceptance, or otherwise, are made. The rabbit on the wrong side of it is doomed - in true fancier words - to be 'Turfed Off'.

This imaginary line will fluctuate according to the officiating judge's reaction on development, up to the age restriction, but all follow in close harmony with one another. The keen, every day fancier is knowledgeable in every move to do with exhibition, they know in their mind, how much the various judges will tolerate in appearance for age, before the 'Axe' is applied. Listen in to pen side chats for enlightenment on the subject; it's a popular topic and you'll hear, 'Judge so and so, will not wear that one', or 'yes it'll get past alright'. Knowing the judge is applicable here, for it has a sobering effect on the number of 'chance it' youngsters one is called on to sort out.

There will always be plenty of border line cases to deal with, especially round about the Young S.S. season, which shows the supporters have confidence in the judge's ability to understand all that is involved in the effort to win. The rising judge should establish early on this 'So far, no further' line, by resolute procedure, it can save much friction in judging.

The theme so far, has centred entirely on the 'Over Developed versus Age' relationship. We ought not to let the direct opposite escape attention. Under developed and under age is just as rife. This condition fails to register its presence with any force and the judge is frequently deluded by size. The little 'Old Un' is a far reaching menace, it competes in young classes until it attains a wizened look to belie its designation. When suspicion is aroused on this score look to the focal points already mentioned, toe nails, etc., if they have taken on real strength in character, your mistrust is well founded. The common saying of bygone years 'The rabbit is as old as it looks' is only partial truth. It may have served the judge of that day as a means of reckoning and given complacency, but time does not stand still. With the advancement in nutritious feeding, out of season breeding, change in breed standards - for better or worse - exhibition practices and regulations, to mention a few, the judge of today must seek out the things more compatible to the whole truth and use them intelligently. Always be firm in action when dealing with this rather delicate task.

The clean cut ruling must be made. The 'Benefit of Doubt' verdict, often in show reports, is not judgement. It savours of the gesture of favouritism to the recipient, as the doubt is still left in abeyance. There should be no room for doubt in the mind of a judge, who is master of the art.

One other troublesome link in the chain of uncertain eligibility, which baffles all judges at sometime, is the rabbit at its transition period in life. We know the limit set qualifying the various breeds to be declared as young stock, but there is a blank space of weeks following when it is 'adolescent' in character. Any age and year bred classes do in a way provide competition for this kind of exhibit, though they have one drawback. Wins under such restriction do not carry the significance in merit, compatible with first prize's collected in young and adult classes. The zealous exhibitor is not over partial to any age and year bred classes, other than perhaps as additional duplicates, for the clause 'wins not to count toward championship honours' may operate. Further, many prudent competitors possessing the well advanced youngster, in fine trim, will not risk the slur of O.D., by entering it in its legitimate young class, but prefers to sacrifice slight odds by allowing it to challenge in the appropriate adult breed class. This is a genuine sporting act and often collects compensatory returns in early autumn, when older stock competing with it has lost bloom from summer showing.

The judges problem with the adolescent type of rabbit in

adult classes and the subsequent action regarding it, can only be really controversial up to about the end of June at the latest. The debatable point arising is, can a rabbit wearing the current year ring be classed as adult?, for if the adult is correctly ringed, it cannot be more than about five to six months in age. The reasoning comes into focus when, and only when, such exhibits finish up by winning the scheduled adult class and its ring number is recorded. If it is placed lower than first then no query or objection transpires, it passes muster as an adult.

Rabbits within the description under discussion, having survived throughout the rigorous examination to reach the ring reading ceremony, have been dismissed from the class on the facts disclosed by its identification mark.

There is a rule which prohibits a young rabbit whose standard specifies the adult age as being 5 months from being shown in an adult class before June 1st. No judge willingly contradicts personal judgement, which is the case if the ring worn by the last exhibit left on the table fails to substantiate basic reckoning, and is allowed to turn virtual victory into defeat.

Here again, as in all judging predicaments, the judge is sole arbitrator, and must 'paddle the canoe of self extrication' out of the dilemma, however blame or praiseworthy the ultimate conclusion arrived at may appear.

At the one short period of time in each year, when the contradiction is most likely to occur, great care should be exercised when judging adult classes. By taking precautions the mind will register, with little hesitation, the contestant's right to inclusion or exclusion. Most judges quickly dispose of all exhibits failing to measure up to the prescribed standard in size and fitness. The comment, 'you're not man enough for this class' is a favourite expression judges deliver, as the rabbit goes back cardless to its pen. The accurate birthday of all exhibits is a truth concealed, and is of no great concern to the judge, whose use of discretionary discrimination in the matter must be acceptable as a substitute. If the rabbit's development adjusts itself up to the approximate grade, and is permitted by the judge to contest its way through the adult class, on this performance it ought not to be denied its claim to senior rank. Marking rings have proved to be a real boon to the rabbit keeping community, they are the means to establish many facts, but they are not entirely conclusive to age or growth rate of the wearer. Ability to stand up to its competitive classification is one main factor taken into consideration in judging, remembering the permissible variation in adultness. We have the YOUNG ADULT, not so robust in build as the MATURE ADULT, which in turn has more vitality and vigour, than the AGEING ADULT. All three have clear division in make up, but qualify under the ADULT heading in competition.

WITHHOLDING PRIZES AND SPECIAL AWARDS

Showing to win, is probably the one great urge to exhibition, but the outcome to expectation is always latent at the time of making entries. If the exhibit entered in competition is of inferior quality to others taking part in the same class, then it fails to win. It may miss the cards altogether, if it encounters lively opposition. In this circumstance, the owner can find the answer to disappointment, perhaps grudgingly, but sufficiently to help resigned acceptance of the appointed lot.

The big shock to exhibitors is when their rabbit is not beaten in a straight fight, yet does not win conclusively. It heads the class but does not collect the 1st prize card. When the motive behind this state of affairs is brought to light, the individual may resent the implication and will not be convinced its fair play within the principle governing show regulation.   There is strong exception to the judge who withholds 1st, 2nd, or any other prize card award from a breed class for the reason 'quality is too far below standard' to merit premier appraisement.

To deprive someone of something they feel is their just due, will bring displeasure as well as varied argument against the decision you've made. You will be told the best rabbit in a poor quality class is entitled to the highest award on offer. It may be pointed out to you that there can be no 2nd if the 1st is missing. The 2nd can only be 2nd to its higher unit.   Furthermore, it is illegal to curtail the orderly sequence in awards, 1st down to commended, because there is no qualitative clause in making entry to compete.

Most people engaged in show business recognise the fact of a contractual undertaking when the Show Secretary accepts entry fees from exhibitors. It gives the entrant a chance to win one of the stipulated money amounts in return. There can be no 'side tracking' on this issue. The B.R.C. show rule fully covers the liability. It states that no prize money shall be withheld and the three best rabbits in a class, irrespective of whether awarded cards or not, shall be paid prize money as advertised. Interpretation of this rule clearly indicates the Red, Blue, Yellow, or any other card colour combination that is used to denote top awards, are symbols of foremost quality in exhibits, closely related to each other in merit. The soundness of the rule quoted is twofold. It renders safe prize money interest of exhibitors and safeguards one true judging precept, which is to uphold worthiness of the exhibit receiving full honours.

The judge has a series of strict moral obligations to the whole rabbit community. The one of particular interest here is in not permitting false conception in 'stock grade' to circulate in the fancy.   Failure to observe this maxim is certain to bring disillusionment to somebody.   So many rabbit keepers and breeders with limited experience in this undertaking have implicit faith in show card records. There is no justifiable reason why this confidence should be shaken on account of flimsy judging.

Most breed specialist clubs give support to Shows these days in the form of 'Certificate of Merit' or its equivalent. They are intended to signify the superior rabbit of the breed concerned. The awarding of such a special is entrusted entirely to the judge's discretion. They have the sole right to give or not to give these additional commendations. Strict observance to the ruling giving sanction to issue or withhold, and rigid adherence to the requirements in the exhibit needed to qualify, is absolutely necessary. If it were otherwise, the complimentary distinction intended becomes spurious and the judges action farcical. To amplify the truth in this last sentence the following illustration is given. The intention is to impress on all judges, great or small, the ill effects resulting if they fail to use their full powers in every judging decision. The British Rabbit Council was at one time unceasingly under barrage from all quarters regarding its Challenge Certificate scheme. It was accused of issuing the means whereby cheap Champions were made. The loud outcry against worthless bits of cardboard and all the other derogatory accompaniments is recent common knowledge to most. If we look at the then C.C. intention fair and square, the root cause of this thoughtless nonsense cannot be charged to the promoters account. The B.R.C. did no more than offer C.C.s conditionally. The condition being precise in meaning, free from confusion. To refresh memory, here it is word for word. I HEREBY CERTIFY that in my opinion the exhibit whose ring number is stated on the reverse is a typical specimen of its breed, without serious fault

and worthy of championship honours. Signed --- Judge.   The
rabbit gaining a B.R.C. championship is required to win five C.C.s
under at least three approved judges, two of whom had to be
recognised by the breed Specialist Club.

Surely these forthright precautionary measures relieved the
promoting body from the wholesale attacks made. If unworthy
Champions existed with such clear instructions in vogue, then the
responsibility for it lay with the judges, who had the final say in the
awarding of them.

That it is unpopular to withhold specials offered for the
specific purpose of praising the extra good specimen, is made
fairly obvious to the withholder whenever it is done. This may be
partially the reason why judges incline to take the least line of
resistance by giving all there is to give, in the hope no real harm
is done to lower the level of ideal quality. While this kind of laxity
in judging pleases the lucky receiver at the time, it is doubtful if
the genuine fancier, on reflection, finally respects or appreciates
pampering of this kind. The pride of achievement is bound to lose
its full satisfaction on realisation of the automatic way it was
obtained.   It is advisable at the commencement of judging, to
check the breeds claiming special attention in regard to the
distinction for meritorious honours.   Use sound exacting
judgement as the various candidates come under scrutiny.
Record your finding at the time in your judging book, for or
against the award. Have no second thoughts about it afterwards,
or permit doubt as to rightful opinion given to cross the mind.
Persuasive overtures to a reconsideration of the adverse deed is
almost certain to come from the person who has a seeming
grievance, but it is fatal even to waver from the course already
adopted.   The judge's decision must always be final, with no
recourse to a further decision. Check details on all Specialist Club
Certificates before signing. If you do this you'll not be guilty of

incautious, doubtful, undeserving gifts, which have the element of deceptive puffery. Above all never sacrifice PRESTIGE for POPULARITY.

SPECIALIST CLUB JUDGES PANELS

All National breed Clubs have their recognised panel of judges, elected annually by the members. These panels are limited in numbers, varying from 12 up to a maximum of 40, according to size of Club and breed popularity. The latter figure mentioned may seem substantial and appear to offer to the person who has started to move in the direction of active judging, a reasonable chance to make a further step forward to the objective. Unfortunately, for the optimist there are always more applicants than vacancies for the exalted positions. To attain Club judge status unopposed is something almost unheard of nowadays. If it did happen, you will have made but little headway towards the ultimate goal. It would bring no significance to the minds of exhibiting public. It is not easy for the young, would be progressive judge to gain access to some of these select circles; the obstacles to surmount are many, which means a concerted resolve to conquer all odds. Even after you've impressed some one section of a club sufficiently, by acts, deeds, deportment, to be nominated for office, you'll still require votes to secure election. The voters are dispersed all over the country. Your claims, however good, may be obscure to many and this will lower the required support. Not a few of the less prominent judges have knocked, hard, loud and long, at the judging panel doors and failed to gain the admittance to recognition which would undoubtedly enhance their judging progress. The unseen 'Imp' set to guard all avenues to these apparent preserves is most difficult to by pass. He seems determined to hold off all but fully approved candidates, and to thwart ambitious desires of junior judges.

To many, this frustration looks like the 'dead end' to aspirations, and bitter comment is often levelled at the panel system. It is condemned as a 'dog in the manger' kind of set up, to provide distinction to those persons thereon. In some ways this contention may be true, if only the bare fact of the inscribed name is taken into account.

One other common grumble from persevering contenders is that a number of elected judges on many panels remain dormant year in, year out, thereby causing obstruction, not only by retarding the active judges possible inclusion, but also restricting the Club members chances.

The scope of Specialist Club support to local Societies must diminish, if part of a judging panel does not fulfil its function, for a win under a Club judge gives a better feeling of satisfaction to the winner, and may carry accreditation to championship, or point collecting, honours. The substance to this sort of discontent is not unreal, but nothing can be done in the matter. Open nominations and unfettered voting cannot fail to bring impartial results, however disappointing to individual nominees. The election to judging panels is open to all who have the right credentials for inclusion. If judges, well past their zenith in practical judging can still command a 'Pride of place' on the panels, by virtue of the respect built up in yeoman service to a Club over past years, then its a fitting tribute in kindly remembrance.

Well nigh every eminent Judge has had to tread the same uphill pathway to potency as the one that besets your advance. The reluctance to vacate voluntarily the dignified position in the circumstance, ought not to be difficult to understand. By holding on steadfast to the small beginning in a judging venture, progress may be slow at first, but your true deserts will come in the end.

The young (in service) judge with initiative, will know how wide a field in breed coverage is contemplated. With few exceptions the entire range is the aim, which will instil endeavour to overcome all hindrances opposing the rise in gradation. It may mean bowing to a condition not meeting personal approval, but so long as it is not an insult to honesty or character the means to an end is justified.

The expanding practice of breed Specialist Clubs insisting that all panel judges must be full members of their organisation is causing concern in the judging fraternity. Should it become universal, this expanding new departure will impose a substantial financial call on the semi-professional judge, who may have from 50 to 90 odd per cent of Specialist Club backing. In the past all round judges (as distinct from breeder judges) on a panel were levied with a small nominal amount to seal their recognition, oft-times ability was a good enough passport. A number of judges in this class feel they give real service to the Club and its members, outside of actual judging, to offset the claim made for the full monetary contribution, and their dignity is ruffled at the thought of having to pay. It is not fully known how much gratuitous overtime is the lot of the judge who has built up a firm reputation on hard study and work. The Specialist Club Secretary requests a contribution to the now-in-fashion periodical breed bulletin, or for the Yearbook. He stresses the wish for strong comments on breed failings with the object of stalling unwanted characters that spoil and detract from the perfect specimen. Individual breeders follow the same course of enquiry, in the hope of gaining information beneficial to future breeding. There is no obligation on the part of a judge to accept these extended services, but few will ignore the favours asked.

The judges views have a goodly support from one side of the fancy but on the other hand there is the opposite school of thought, who, by the trend in present events might well have the ascendancy.

Those in full support of the compulsory rule maintain that everyone in receipt of Club benefits ought to contribute equally with members, to maintain financial balance. They believe that the panel behind the judge is sound advertisement for the qualified, and acts as an inducement to Show Committees to engage such a personality. Further force to the argument is levied on B.R.C. action. This body is blamed for the lead to the provision, but the analogy is not a fair one. The only way it can exercise control over possible malpractice in awards is to insist that the judge comes within their jurisdiction by full membership, before acting on their behalf. No affiliated Club or Society is refused supporting benefits, when straight forward conditions exist. In fact, almost unlimited patronage is in operation. Specialist Clubs' limited judging panels, make a vast difference and the comparison is not equal.

To sum up the situation from both sides, the analysis brings out mutual concessions, having a two way application with possible loss and gain to either side. A few judges in the past made it their custom to pay the Club Subscription as a tribute, after being elected to its judging panel, the reverse to this is not so palatable. While the tried and trusted Judge may be able to hold out from an enforced, believed imposition, it is doubtful if the 'Aspiring Judge' will have any other choice but to accept the prescribed ruling. Individualism characterises judging and all its associates. Judges have just one or two 'Gentlemen's Agreements' between them, but no organised arrangement in working routine as a collective protection from the things that may rankle, so each individual must fight alone the conflicts of conscience in all matters controversial, liable to effect one's judging prospects.

COMBINED JUDGING

The main duplicate classes, Breeders, Challenge, Grand Challenge, and usually one or two other special ones are judged jointly at all Shows where more than one judge is employed. It is not so long ago that at the big classics, all the judges engaged participated in the climatic end, vieing with each other for the spoils of distinction, with small regard to ethics. The number of judges clustered round the table often times reached double figures and as each was primarily interested in only one or two exhibits in the hunt, it developed into a battle of wits between the judges, each striving to jockey their favourites into leading positions, and casting aside sane, balanced judgement. The more conscientious type of judge taking part thought the issue too much of a gamble, foreign to calm reasoning, and found very little satisfaction in the association, notwithstanding that the major proportion of the rabbits brought forward in these scrambles were high in quality. They felt helpless to stem spectacular actions from ousting genuine judging. In fact, many times a judge retired from the fray to register strong dislike with this display of tactics. Happily, the B.R.C.'s revised Show Rule, 'Not more than three judges shall judge jointly in any one class', has brought the situation into better keeping with what is at stake. This rule makes it possible for big show Promoters to arrange their programme of duplicate classes by discretionary use of judges at their disposal. It enables them to team up a combination of knowledgeable, levelheads, who can preserve equanimity among themselves, which in turn protects each breed duplicated from prevailing exploitation, with a fair-field to all.

With due regard to the welcome betterment resulting from the present system, joint judging is still the most delicate form one has to deal with. Not only does it require attentive contemplation on your part, the estimations arrived at must coincide within fractional distance to that of your colleagues. Sometimes all will be plain sailing; unanimity will be accomplished with ease, free from debate between the three working together. But identical interpretation in the exhibits excellence will not hold sway in the majority of cases. A mild clash in opinions is bound to come and this is where the test in cool, collected deliberation arises, if you are to act up to full responsibility, which is simply, fair, honest, calculated judgement in accord with the other two. Be conciliatory in reasoning together, it goes a long way to even out small opposing deductions.

A little chaffing may be going on, when two or three judges gather round a table to carry out this kind of judging. Some who overhear these brief exchanges, may think it caustic and derogatory to one another. But at no time take this cross chat at face value, its just one of those things some judges indulge in after long intimate acquaintance at the job. If you're a newcomer to trio judging and meet this banter, don't let it fluster you, 'in one ear out of the other' is good advice, until you can sum up it's intention correctly.

It is a rarity in threesome judging for a state of deadlock to be reached, two will invariably see eye to eye on the one exhibit. This is sufficient to clinch the placing. If you happen to be the odd one out, take it in kindly spirit, show no resentment at being over-ruled, as usually it is only one or two scoring points separating universal agreement, due to personal emphasis on a small dislike, which does not register as high in the estimate of your co-judges.

It will happen that many exhibits coming up in these duplicate classes have been judged and placed separately by all three judges at some time through the day, in breed and limited sectional duplicate classes. Each judge will know how his order was cast, and the reason for it. Two judges may not have seen or handled each other's exhibits before and may have dissenting views on the placings. One might prefer a change round, the rabbit put second, above the first, or one breed ahead of another, but each judge must respect former individual actions.

The reversal of placings is not rampant in collective judging, but it will thrust up its head now and again to ruffle feelings. Always be charitable if the situation threatens. A variety of things can produce a changed aspect from the original deductions made by the one judge, when two others go over the same material hours later. Failing light, a little less thoroughness by skipping finer points; it can be that the two judges are more close associates in personal preferences, which do not strike the first judge so forcefully. Like and dislike cannot be entirely eliminated from rabbit judging. Tolerance to each other's previous action, when judging together, with a mind to give a little, take a little, will work wonders in co-ordination.

No matter how staid or steadfast is the judge's intention to be impartial, personal taste in some small attraction can unconsciously encroach in the process of sorting through the exhibits. It is a force to which there is no answer, a human frailty seen in others, not in ourselves, but all the same, it counts against the trend of three minds leading to one conclusive agreement in triple judging. This truth should be reconcilable to all judges. No two judges have the right to shift another's line of following exhibits, unless there has been a grave, unmistakable, error in justice. Then, and only then, should the position be rectified. To do it on a simple fancied footing is unjustifiable conduct. When three judges are working together in this manner, and rabbits, to which neither have had previous dealings, come under their mandate, give them equal consideration with all the rest, they should carry no forfeit as new contenders. There is a tendency for attention to drift in favour of the rabbits that have climbed to the 'higher places', through the hands of operating judges, by way of straight and intersection duplicate classes.

DUAL JUDGING

On the surface, this may seem almost identical with the last heading, but it is more open to conflict than the former, in that the third person is missing, who, in a large measure plays the role of referee, and is able to clinch a settlement in favour of one, or the other nominee, to relieve a deadlock. The bulk of our provincial Shows engage but two judges. The constitution is quite well known, Fancy Judge, Fur Judge. They come together in the final classes and it is at this stage that a tussle with equal convictions on both sides is likely, resulting in a stalemate situation.

When you are confronted with this sort of crisis, examine yourself to make sure obstinacy has not temporarily replaced cool, calm, judgement. This vice is more in being than is generally supposed and is a matter for hard self-discipline. Another supposition that lingers in the mind of some judges is that they must push and stick to their personal nomination for the topmost awards in duplicate classes, regardless of all the challenging qualities brought forward by the second judge. Many exhibitors also hold this view, and are not backward in making it known, which might in a few instances have influential suggestion to this particular dogma. This precept is all wrong. It is certainly not judging within the true meaning, it rather points to imprudence and headstrong priggishness. There's no disgrace or loss of dignity in giving way to the co-judge's preference, if you're convinced it is the better rabbit. The best, agreed exhibit, must always scale to the highest place. It is of no consequence which of two judges is responsible for it's advent to the class.

The time will come however when neither judge can see the way clear to capitulate to the other's point of view on the claims of each exhibit. Instinctively, both will know there is no hope of trying to break through the barriers of dissension or tactfully continuing persuasive efforts to convince to one way of thinking. Provided there is a strong common parity in relative excellence involved then the judges at cross purpose should not be accused of stubbornness or of seeking self glorification at the expense of the partner in the hazard. The judge's training calls for firm, decisive, unalterable, conclusions, from any examination.

This fact, develops the tense situation of no yielding by either party from time to time, when rivalry in opponents is equally convincing.

You will likewise have to bear with obvious ridiculous opposition in the quest for rightful awards. This may be thought a blatant narrative to set down, but its one unaccountable lapse in the judge's calendar that is hard to comprehend. When met with, it just takes the ground from beneath one's feet. In the light of experience one might say the cause is most often through limited knowledge of the breeds, lack in judging stability, usually due to restricted, practical activity, on the part of one judge. It may spring from sudden impulse to produce an air of 'Assertive Impression', owing to tension of the occasion. Undefined conflicts of this nature disturb the true technicality in judging and are not expedient to the service.

The regular judges, when working together in pairs, show little inclination to compromise in a tight struggle for priority choice, but they seldom combat with each other if plain evidence, divides their respective contestants. Moreover, the well seasoned judge should not ride the high horse over a junior member, when trying to 'Bamboozle' a favourable way out of rational opposition, by adopting the attitude of superior authority, to the disparagement of the less prominent. It is a callous action that might well undermine the confidence of someone striving to make good as a judge. Anyone who indulges in this mannerism, however unintentional, should reflect back to personal early efforts to consolidate a footing on the judging ladder.

Snobbish treatment is nothing new in the annals of the business, most of today's celebrities have been victims of this behaviour from some reigning notable, and well know its effect on morale. All disagreements, genuine or contemptible, which bring judging progress to a complete standstill have but a single solution. It is the calling in of a third party to act as adjudicator.

This appointment, at the request of the dissentients, lays with the Show Secretary or Manager, but it is up to both judges to be content with the person commissioned to adjudicate, before the act occurs. The B.R.C. rule covering the action merely states that when the Judges are unable to agree, the Show Committee, or Secretary acting on their behalf, must appoint an umpire who must not be an exhibitor at that show of the breed or breeds to be judged by him (or in the case of a Specialist club the exhibits) and other than at a Specialist club must be a B.R.C. member. His decision shall be final.

Whilst compliance with this order may be beyond question, other precautions are necessary to steer clear of unsuspected pitfalls, that can - and do - lead on to later protests.

The umpire must not have an interest in the Show as an exhibitor. No one is permitted this dual privilege however pressing the need is to terminate the dispute. There ought not to be direct sympathetic connecting interests at stake to sway the outcome, such as intimate association with one owner and stock, their creditable history in performance and so forth. Neither should know animosity on the part of the mediator, to either breed or breeder be given the chance to interfere in the straight passage of separating the two exhibits. It is not easy to avoid the personality complex when wanting an intermediary judge at the small show, as it is more or less area contained. But the two judges at shortlived variance, should in all round fairness, discretely enquire as to the competency and moral bearing, of the one to intervene, if credentials are unknown.

The handing over to a substitute of the problem does not exclude the right of the dissentients to disregard ways and means whereby the crisis is ended. Their responsibility is still to see that the law in judging impartiality operates. When amicable concord is reached in this, the one deputed, must be a free agent. No explaining from the judges on the why's and wherefore's of the disruption, no sung praises to approve either exhibit. The division of the two exhibits must take an unimpeded course.

The ultimate pronouncement can only be right for one of the two anxious judges. If you gain advantage over your fellow judge, show no marked elation in victory. If the reverse is your lot, and you must suffer in defeat, do it with a smile, in silence, for crowing and moaning are both bad irritants, best out of dual judging.

COMMENDABLE ACTION

The partisan spirit toward judges is a thing that should be fostered at all times. Disparagement is too often the subject of conversation in judging circles, which is sure to be overheard by outsiders who listen in. If it is slighting another's competency, it is passed on wholesale as a 'tit-bit', losing nothing in transit to tone down exaggeration. It has already been pointed out elsewhere how perfect unity in mind, thought and deed, cannot exist in judging, so we must forbear with each other in the things not to exact mutual interpretation, to preserve a measure of connecting respect between judges.

One form of trap to beware of, is the sought condolence of someone disappointed with their lot under another judge. A rabbit may be brought to you with formal request for comment on its quality, you will be quite safe in assuming that it has not done too well in its breed class.

Do not be tempted to commiserate with the one looking for consolation by trumpery exposition, supporting the idea that it ought to have gained higher awards. This will provoke further hostility to the act done by the actual judge. Extravagant praise thus given, is most liable to start a round of peevish complaint and to end in the playing off of one judge's decision, made in a true judgimg situation against the superfluous statement, made in one which is not..

There is only one ethical way of dealing with this type of disgruntled exhibitor. Decline to meddle in a colleague's personal arrangement of exhibits, by making no inferential remarks likely to delude the one, or discredit an associate. Simply refer all questioners and questioning of this kind, back to the responsible judge, who alone knows the correct answer to fanciful dissatisfaction. After all, each judge should be no more than 'Captain of his own ship'.

If good fellowship were the order of the day, with all back biting 'taboo', it would bring the judges more closely together. As a better united body they could do far more constructive work in their active sphere, if only by compiling acceptable standards in decorum, covering a small multitude of things subsidiary to the ultimate judging of exhibits. This in itself would tend to raise the moral standing of judges in the fancy, and would probably save much idle, critical chatter, heard from all sorts and condition of people in the Fancy.

ENGAGEMENTS IN PROSPECT

Be prompt in your reply to Show Secretaries enquiring for judging services, whether you can accept the engagement or not. Always quote your terms clearly if you're free to meet the invitation, so there's no misunderstanding or shock at settling time, after completion of your duties. When you reply to a request to judge at any Society or Club event, you are also entitled to ask for reciprocal quick consideration in decision, with early notification of the position, one way or the other.

Booking and fixing engagements can be a tricky business. Unavoidable complications butt in, and the big tantaliser occurs when more than one request is received to tender as judge at separate Shows to be held on the same day.

The difficulty here lays in the fact that having just despatched an offer to one Society, what is the answer to the second. Does one make the same straight forward approach in answering by return, temporarily forgetting about having already entered into partial commitment elsewhere, or hang on, in the hope of a speedy enlightenment - yea or nay - on the first committal. It is a temptation to have two strings to your bow, in case the first offer is, in the end, declined; but you do risk being landed with a couple of Shows to judge on the one day if you go ahead heedlessly. If this happens - and it has - you are then forced to admit double booking to one party involved, and dodge the entanglement, by hook or by crook. This will provoke annoyance - the minimum reaction to expect - from the injured Society, who will put a big black mark to your name. This cannot be easily cancelled out to bring you back into their good favour and further consideration to seek your co-operation in judging.

The alternative of 'wait and see' how you fare with the first show before doing anything with the second, may leave you with neither in hand. Non-acceptance of the first advance and lengthy delay in notice to this effect, could mean forfeiture of a chance, owing to the lapse in time, to contract with the enquiry held in suspension. The Show Committee, waiting for a reply, gain the impression that you are not interested in their Show affairs, or they may be a little impatient to secure judging services, so they appoint another judge who submitted a firm tender on the dot.

In the past, some judges did try to obviate the intervening time-lag, by setting a limit to the duration of keeping open the date applied for, and accepted pro-tem, but it had no effective bearing on the trouble. Confirmatory acceptances still came a few days late, with perhaps an apology and an excuse. If the judge had to stick to the time limit rider, through taking another engagement right on the dead-line of his time limit, then there was resentment on the part of the unfortunate one in default, to the seeming high-handedness from a judge.

To be bound down in exactness is antagonistic to rabbit organisations in general; a little latitude is always taken as granted.

Of course, the snags set out do not accompany every solicitation received, far from it, many will be all 'plain sailing' to negotiate, free from complication. When two, even three fold invitations crowd in for the same date, the safe method for the judge to employ is to clear one tentative transaction completely before embarking on to a second. You will then avoid raising false hope, disappointment, dissatisfaction and muddles, and it will certainly relieve the mind of much anxiety in keeping clear from embarrassing parallel undertakings, which could be harmful to your reputation. On balance nothing much is lost in bookings, by adhering to this system. Should you have to temporarily default in expeditious response to requests for your talent, on account of priority offering, never fail to give the true reason for the delay in your letter of explanation, however late it might be in despatch. Genuine frankness in apology for the apparent neglect will usually put you right with the club concerned.

PRUDENT PRECEPTS

It is the unregarded, insignificant, minor things connected with judging, that lead to strained relations and indignant feeling toward the judge, especially when neighbouring rabbit associations are drawn into an unsuspected quandary over what might be termed 'judge's indiscretions'. Care must be exercised before accepting each judging appointment, by referring back to those already fixed, so as not to appear in the same immediate locality at too close an interval.

There is no other restriction to a quick reappearance in the area than the code of 'Judicious conduct'. This, if unheeded, may have harmful repercussion in the judge's renown, also the show receipts. It would be a bit bumptious on the part of a judge to assume personage is the supreme motive behind all judging invitations sent out, and when received, if free, to take on the engagement without more ado. The judge's value to a Club is viewed by its committee and members as an attraction to induce exhibitors support by way of entries made in full confidence and unhampered by doubts.

Both value and support can drop with a bump, if the judge has not the foresight to be discreet in movement, consistent to all common interests. So many near rival associations are secretive in their early planning and neglect to exchange details of intentions or certainties with one another, which might forestall a clash in Show enterprises. The Society catering for the not far removed second visit, would have much concern for the success of their venture having engaged the judge in all good faith only to find out about the earlier fixture when too late to sheer off from the identical sameness. It would be an error to knowingly have the repetition judge for it could upset their calculated support no end. The bulk of entries come to the moderate size show from within an easily accessible radius. The lower and unplaced exhibits at the first venue could hardly be expected to turn up in strength at the second, for a possible repeat defeat. Their absence would probably greatly reduce the over-all total entry, and the judge, through the inconsiderate act pointed out, would be held to be to blame for the downfall.

The judge must be wary and steer away from this danger by being alert when filling in vacant dates.

The judge's duty, when a second class consecutive service is sought, is to let the trailing Club know of the already arranged nearby visit. This will absolve you from all ulterior motive likely to bring about trouble and will give them the right to retract the invitation which they usually do with grateful thanks for your thoughtfulness.

On a few occasions when intimation of this particular circumstance is sent to a Society in ample time, they may, if you stand high in their esteem, suggest a way round the obstacle, by arranging their schedule so that your classes do not coincide with those judged at the neighbouring Show. Naturally, such concessionary gestures will depend on your judging qualifications and the number of judges being employed. If the renewed request to judge comes in this manner, have no qualms in meeting it, the follow up has been given you full sanction.

The whole system to do with engagements entered into, relies on the goodwill of contracting Clubs and judges. They are usually made far in advance of the specified date, yet few fail to materialise satisfactorily. It is considered a grave breach in behaviour for either side to break faith, by recanting during the interim period, without indisputable, legitimate reasons. Mutually agreed release may be authorised at times, on the grounds of some hardship, but the releasing party will often feel to have been badly let down, more so if it be a Club or Society who will have to find a substitute judge, with perhaps some difficulty. The judge is most often the culprit in seeking this concession, with a view to transferring his services higher up the scale in limelight and dignity.

We all know the lure of appointment to the Specialist Club annual Stock Shows and the pride experienced in being elected to officiate at one of these, and how galling it is to be debarred from the 'glory' by some other pledge for the same day.

'Look before you leap' fits in here, with the judge who keeps one eye open for this kind of main chance. You may have enhanced your standing in one direction by altering course, only to harm it elsewhere. It is true that a Society may acquiesce in a plea for release, but it does not always mean condonation for leaving them in the lurch.

The judge should honour every show undertaking, at all costs. It is never worthwhile trying to play fast and loose with a Show Committee on account of a more alluring fixture being offered - just too late. Reliance and stability in a judge ranks high with engaging bodies, and in the long run their preservation will pay handsome dividends.

The peak periods in each Show season brings to the progressing judge a miniature inundation of over-lapping invitations to place awards. Having passed through one such rush, reflection on it may tempt the judge into being selective in accepting judging engagements when there will be possible choice by a little marking time. If you're out to offer widespread judging service to the Fancy, the sensible plan is to book the first Show applying for any free date you may have. Do not discriminate by letting a Table Show, potential, go by, in the hope that a Pen Show will come along to take its place - it may not. A bird in the hand is worth two in the bush, and its unwise to think you can pick and choose the Shows to judge. If you attempt to, you'll be caught up in hesitation and fall between two stools.

The aim of the judge, once under way, must be to build up a commanding position in the rabbit world; to grow from almost insignificance to rubbing shoulders with the upper ten. This is done in gradual stages, and by methodical, uniform, deliberate, frank and sound actions, treating all Shows with uniformity.

The standing of the show, classic, big, not so big open afternoon or evening table show, is secondary to the judge's function; the same intense concern in judging must be applied to all. Do not compromise your ability by being slip shod over exhibits at the limited local Club gathering, which is the training and try out ground in preparation of most things to do with exhibition. Believe it or not, the judge ripe in experience can at times gain something fresh to store for future use at even the smallest of shows, if the highest exertion is expended. As far as one can see, judging education is destined never to be fully complete. The hitherto unperceived condition produced by progress in breeding of even the long established breeds, will register for better or worse with the observant judge, and stimulate watchfulness for the gradual change in fashions going on all the time.

When the judge's 'ism's' cease to reverberate to further insight to the calling, and he feels that all there is to know in rabbit technique is known, then its time for him to rest on the laurels earned through past diligence - in retirement.

REMUNERATIVE REWARD

This is a thorny topic of divided opinions and outlook throughout the rabbit community, with the judges who know the complete answer to mercenary accusation thrown at them now and again, mainly keeping their own council. It may have been wise to let this controversial subject take care of itself, but it is of major importance to the whole thesis and must be given air.

In making out a good case from the judges' viewpoint, comparison with other monetary aspects applicable to the industry cannot be avoided but all inferences are free from malice and rancour.

The financial receipts for judging in the main only affect the judges regularly, almost continually, in demand, who go about the country and those with a mind to graduate to such a position.

To the later section a warning must be given. Have no delusions as to the income derived from judging. If you're thinking in terms of a livelihood, abandon it at once. Taken over a season's working, the net return in cash for time and energy expended, will not stand close investigation as compatible to the lowest commercial rate of payment in industry.

The top rank judges are all temperate in their charges, and the scale is quite common knowledge. Two guineas fee, plus expenses, with the expenses invariably being kept down to bare rail fare and over night accommodation if the distance warrants it.

[Note, in 1992 this would be about £20 but fees are today very much more variable than they were].

It is admitted that the expenses item is a drain on the Society's resources, and the total charge in some instances is steep, but they have usually counted the cost before picking their judge. The judges who respond to far and wide invitations are not unmindfull of this heavy burden - if some of the stories of night trips, unearthly early hour starts and thoroughly uncomfortable conditions encountered in the interest of expense economy were made public, most of them would be treated as fiction.   But whatever the extra amount added to fee in this way, it is no asset to the judge. It is simply repayment of his expenses.

It does not need the mind of a great statistician to work out the number of shows the judge would have to do to obtain a respectable living, or the impossibility of coping with the figure deduced.   To judge 100 shows in a year is a target few judges can reach. If a judge does this number then a proportion of Table Shows at about half the fee mentioned must be taken into calculation.   The truth is that rabbit judging is not all that lucrative

To check its financial returns with everyday commercial undertaking gives an unfavourable balance.

However, the modest fee paid for this key service to a Show is the tie that binds reciprocal obligation, with maximum assurance that the promise will stand firm.   If it were not customary, judging transactions formerly agreed might be precarious as to completion.   It obviates a change in mind at the last minute by the judge.   Reimbursement is one incentive to carry out judging bargains made, when one would like to slide out of it gracefully, or on a weak pretence, to do something more congenial and beneficial to personal gratification.

There is little doubt that the fee is responsible for the safe reliable announcements by the Society as to who will sign or initial judging slips at their event. It could be anything but certain, if judging relied on honorary precept with only the bond of good will as surety for the judge's attendance. It also helps to back up the fine standing record in judging circles of very little defaulting on engagements, except through illness, as the fee to be paid carries the right to compensatory payment if default occurs, and the reason put forward in defence is deemed frivolous.

The judge who is not beholden to remuneration in any shape or form and declines to accept it, can escape from the rigour of semi-compulsory regularity at will. This independence allows freedom in action all along the judging line. Whereas the fee receiving judge is bound by convention, which makes the dependence more equal and reassuring on both sides.

The school of thought that rabbit-keeping, with all its pursuits is a hobby, and as such, all judging, for one thing, ought to be carried out gratis, is a fair stretch of imagination and often wishful thinking. Looking at the exhibition side in a general way - there is always exception to be found - money looms large in calculation from all quarters.

The judge's fee is only equal to the benefits derived from showing by others participating therein. Successful exhibitors do not pass on winning stock, or progeny bred from it to others, for a mere song. Neither are Champion Bucks placed at stud free of charge to any Does that people like to send for mating. A casual glance down the fancy press advertisments in these two commodities will disperse the pure hobby theory. In fact some price quotations strongly hint at the very reverse.

Judges' names are coupled with a few of these offerings, presumably to add a fillip to encourage the sale or use of stud service, which implies that judges' opinions as shown by their show decisions, are worth exploiting, and does carry weight outside the exhibition scene. No harm is done, neither is a liberty taken with this style of advertisement, for judges themselves hand out many unsolicited testimonials to breeders and their stock while on the round of Shows.

Someone failing to reach expectation in the prize list, asks the judge why and where high position was lost. On unfolding the deficiencies in qualities, the request for a suggested remedy follows, and the recommendation to get a mating from here or fresh blood from there goes out, based on methodical observation and memory of where the suitable outcross to rectify the faults is to be found. Later on, thanks for both advice and recommend may reveal a two-fold appreciation for the intermediary act. This is only one instance of judges' usefulness outside their strict official capacity.

Quite a number of small deeds done, in liaison and advisory form prove to be beneficial to fanciers of all grades. The incidental details to do with judging provide plenty of homework for the judge who is continually out and about, its significance is known only to those doing it. Open Shows are news, and the one medium giving information to rouse widespread interest in current performances of exhibits, bringing up-to-date intelligence to what is going on throughout the country, is the judge's full show report. The compiling for publication of these reports may be considered as part of the judge's duties - they are accepted as such by them - but the task they set is lost sight of by calculators in counting up how long the judge is employed. The glamour of the judging table is not the finish, as many suppose. To go through, check, sort and prepare the data, plus writing up a suitable foreword, will take two to three hours of concentration, with the mind travelling back over the classes as judged, to recreate faded impression, for one should take pains to be accurate in written comment.

Enough has been said to indicate how much the judges figure in show life and its subsidiary followings. Seeing that they're instrumental to collective, individual, meritorious and material successes, their contribution to the circuit of rabbit welfare receives no more pecuniary reward than many other leading associates engaged in breeding, supplying or owning stock capable of winning honours at the Shows.

JUDGES PROSPECTIVE

Judges come, Judges go, the Shows go on as ever. With this continuous routine in motion, there will always be room in the circle for the serious minded would-be judge, bent on securing a sure niche, somewhere about the treetop, in judging prominence. The rise to recognition can only be gradual and much depends on how hard one is willing to work for the desired distinction. Wishing for the Judge's star is an idle dream, bringing no advancement in its direction.

You must study with a retentive mind the full progressional tract, from A to Z as applied to judging. Don't be afraid to check from the Standards Book. There are always new breeds being introduced that you have to have a very good memory of all the standards when it comes to the really finer points, their faults and disqualifications. With a sound knowledge of all technicalities and the natural skill to handle stock correctly - the two are inseparable in appreciative adjudication - you will be well fitted to forge ahead on every occasion that presents itself. The chance to make a bold step forward comes when least expected. If you're prepared, it can be taken in cool confidence, to increase status and give proof of competence. Solidity in all matters affecting the judge's operative function is a great asset toward reaching the summit of ambition.

FINALLY

No judge, in making awards can hope to please more than a few exhibitors at any one time. A number will always disagree with the results of your ultimate conclusions. If you have made these in accord with the dictates of conviction, on balanced qualities, after thorough examination, no one will seriously quarrel with you, but they'll recognise and accept the honest opinion given. Be strictly just to your own conscience, favour neither breed, breeder, or exhibitor, when carrying out official duty, and you will win applause for unswerving services rendered to the rabbit Fancy as a judge.

COMMENTS ON SOME JUDGING PRACTISES.

Various points which have become much more common in recent years and which are subject to considerable debate include:

1   Judges exhibiting in a different show held at the same venue where they are judging on that day. The B.R.C. Rules have changed from time to time and currently allow a judge to exhibit at another show to that which he is judging at the same venue on the same day. The arguments in favour are that a judge judging particularly a small number of exhibits in which there is no connection to his own, does not 'miss' a day of exhibiting, particularly at his specialist club show for example.   The arguments against are that it may distract a judge from his primary duty of judging and in the view of some it is not consistent with the high standards required of a judge.

2   The lack of, or insufficient, reporting in Fur & Feather. A rule has recently been introduced that the reporting of a show is obligatory and unless there are some grounds to prevent it the report must be despatched within a certain period. It must also be said that occasionally the reasons for non-reporting have been that the reports are not always published, which has in the past unhappily been true.

3   Judges not insisting upon seeing all animals which are entered in classes which they are engaged to judge. That is to say, usually, in the judging of duplicate classes where they rely solely upon nominations from other judges thus having very few exhibits out.

Allied to this there have been cases of judges asking for nominations from other judges in order that they do not have to have all exhibits in a class onto the table. They then proceed to judge a very limited proportion of their class, for they bring onto the table only their own winners and also the winners of the classes they have not judged, these being supplied by the other judges.

Whilst one can have a certain amount of sympathy with a judge who does this when he has been asked to judge a class which may be very large indeed [and of course the duplicate classes always come towards the end of the day when other classes have been finished] there is no question that he is both forgetting his obligations to the exhibitors who have entered under him and breaching completely B.R.C. Show Rule number 95 which quite categorically states that the judge must examine all the exhibits as numbered in his judging book.. [and].. see that they are placed before him by the stewards...

There is a second reason for this practice. That is that undoubtedly both judges concerned wish to avoid the chance of cross judging. That is to say they wish to avoid the chance that one judge will select an exhibit which was beaten by another exhibit in the class under the other judge.

Two points can be made concerning this. The first is that if the present system of nominations is to be continued then at least the exhibits placed in the three first places should be nominated to the other judge, and if the third placed winner comes into the cards in the duplicate class, then the judge of that class should call for the exhibit placed reserve, and so on. There have been numerous cases in which the second and the third winners in a class have been placed above the winners in other classes.

The second point is that if the system of nominations

is to continue then the B.R.C. Show Rule relating to the matter should be changed and it should be recognised that in all schedules an explanation that nominations will be made by all judges must be incorporated.

These points do not of course relate to those cases in which, for example, B. I. S. is judged by a judge specially appointed to accept nominations from other judges or from each section from which he is to select the winner.

4   An increasing tendency for judges, when judging duplicate classes with other judges, to push the winning exhibit in their class or classes against all other exhibits no matter what their quality. This practise has become so prevalent that judges talk frequently in their judging reports of 'their' exhibit winning best of section or best in show etc.

These judges would in no way condone 'jockeying' by exhibitors at their table. Indeed many judges will completely pass an exhibit if the jockeying is too blatant. Pushing their own exhibit in a duplicate class with other judges is however a very blatant form of jockeying of the worse kind with even less justification then jockeying by an exhibitor.

In the case of single breed judges it may be argued that the reason a judge will stick to his own winner through thick and thin is that he may know little about the other breeds and is therefore hesitant to judge them. He may know that his own exhibit is a good one and therefore sticks to it. Some might say that he should not be judging a very mixed duplicate class.

The idea that a judge is judged by exhibitors to be good, or indeed the best of the judges in the show,if the exhibit he picked out in his section to be the best goes on to win further honours is the of course nonsense and should be thoroughly exploded.

A judge who insists upon pushing his own exhibit

without regard to the qualities of the other exhibits is a very poor judge indeed.

5   A sole purely specialist judge insisting upon judging duplicate classes thus causing ill feeling. This problem is partly eliminated by the introduction of a new show rule that makes it mandatory for the duplicate class judges to named prior to the show.

6   The final point concerns cross judging. Some judges take to the limit what they consider a moral responsibility to other judges, to ensure that there is no cross judging thus tending to totally overlook their responsibilities to exhibitors which is their prime responsibility.

Almost certainly the reason for some of these laxities in judging practises arise because of the shortness of the usual apprenticeship of judging at the present time.

If one returns to the early periods of training judges it certainly was that the apprenticeship period lasted a number of years and was followed by a period in which, when any person was permitted to judge he was only permitted to judge at very minor shows or as a very junior judge at major shows for a second fairly long period.

The integrity of the judges was a very highly thought of at that period and resulted in the almost total prohibition of the practises which now can cause concern.